Tristan

John Watson

Tristan

Tristan
ISBN 978 1 76109 420 0
Copyright © text John Watson 2022

First published 2022 by
Ginninderra Press
PO Box 3461 Port Adelaide 5015
www.ginninderrapress.com.au

Contents

Introduction	7
Part One	9
Part Two	31
Part Three	45
Part Four	63
Part Five	75
Part Six	91
Part Seven	113
Part Eight	131
Part Nine	153
Part Ten	167
Part Eleven	187

Introduction

Of the earliest texts of the Tristan story, several are long fragments. That of Béroul begins at the famous scene at the pool in the orchard, and ends well before Tristan's last departure from Cornwall. The intervening pages are fortunately intact. That of Thomas is badly scattered into fragments although the ending is preserved. Joseph Bédier proposed an archetype, a poem of considerable length on which the surviving versions could be partly overlaid. Whether the entire version was ever written and subsequently lost, or existed only as a large aggregate in the oral tradition, is of course impossible to say.

This archetype of Bédier's, the 'complete' story from before Tristan's birth to his death, suggested the present work. This attempt was also fired by affection for Béroul and regret at its substantial lost beginning and end. I have therefore worked predominantly from Bédier's reconstruction, then from Béroul, and finally from Thomas, using these sources chiefly as a possible synopsis of events.

Whereas Béroul is written in a long sequence of uninterrupted rhyming couplets – uninterrupted that is by division into verses – I have preferred the model of the old *chansons de geste* in which verses or 'laisses' of variable length divide the action into scenes. I chose the octasyllabic line or, rather, tetrameters, mainly to avoid the florid dangers of the pentameter and as a homage to the lightness, transparency, 'simplicity' of Béroul (where that word must be qualified perhaps by remarking that I prefer Béroul to the later more elaborate Gottfried). Each of the verses is rhymed, or uses half rhyme. Since rhyme in English can easily become obtrusive, particularly in regular patterns, I have used a large variety of patterns from verse to verse which the reader may if he wishes discern. A few could be mentioned: variants on a single rhyme; couplets; rhymes radiating from a central point; various strophic forms; the expanding network where, eventually, every line is matched.

On the matter of metrics, the reader's indulgence – or assistance – is asked, to allow the name 'Tristan' to be pronounced (and thus stressed) as required, either as in English or as in French.

Part One

*The tale of Tristan and the thrall
Of circumstance, whose Chemical,
Embracing chance, chose them; their frail*

*Compliance with contingency;
Events which cast their curious light
On pale Iseut, no longer free;*

*Determined Accident appears,
Sees her and dreaming seizes her;
With Tristan's chains her destiny*

*Is interlinked in forging heat;
The irreversibility
Of passage through entailing years;
Their trace across these towering seas.*

❧

1

As all things precious in the earth –
The gold of vanished kings, or all
Our unrecovered histories,
Or fallen pages from Béroul –
Have long lain hidden from our gaze,
So all that follows, hesitant,
Adduced with contradictions, tears
And smiles and puzzling metaphors,
Frail similes, such figures as
Raise incidents above ideas,
All happened long ago. Beneath
Two trees which tangled overhead
King Mark was welcoming Rivalen
Who came at Cornwall's urgent word.

2

Receiving Cornwall's desperate plea,
Not waiting for the tide, in haste
Crossing the dark, cerulean sea
Came Rivalen from Lyonesse
To aid King Mark in Cornwall lest
By envious enemies his land
Is all laid waste. Thus, to this end,
In battle bravely, side by side,
They rout the rancorous enemy;
They sough and scythe and sigh through them
And then return to castle air
Rejoicing at the banquet board.
There skies of flame and oriflamme
Give way to smiling, fair Blanchefleur.

3

The torrent of events which flows
Still endlessly since Time's first days
When all was chaos in the spheres
Has cast up one who slowly rows
Slanting across its flood. He sees
A mirror bright with certainties,
The lady Blanchefleur rich in sighs.
He reaches land. Then, shipping oars,
He steps ashore. There, in her eyes,
Lie brimming future destinies.
He fights beside her brother, knows
In victory sweet and glorious ease.
And Blanchefleur blushes when she hears
Mark heap on Rivalen high praise.

4

As Rivalen with Blanchefleur stood,
Crowned by the pealing bells' cascade
A minstrel improvising cried
— *Cornwall now lies with Lyonesse*
In holy, sensual embrace.
Let all good people here rejoice.
The sea which wets the ghostly hands
Of thoughts and memories and desires,
Breaks gently on our favoured lands
And writes these names across their shores.
Let night smile on their marriage bed,
And plait them in a single braid.

5

Scarce deliquescent in their love,
Still turned to consummation's grove,
Not quite lost in its leafy path
Which leads them on through all the earth,
They hear the seneschal return
Who had with torches lately brought
Them to their curtained marriage bed
And now will sever with the sword
Of fateful news this ardent night:
Duke Morgan even now lays siege
To Lyonesse, the heart, the crown
Of Rivalen's fair lands at large.

6

King Mark stands at the harbour wall
With Blanchefleur in the sudden pall
Of parting. Sadly they watch the ships,
Still little more than ghostly shapes,
Prepare to leave for Brittany.
The swell was brooding sullenly
And dawn had not yet touched the sea.
Smoke circled from a headland fire.
A few sea birds invisible
Below the cliffs sounded farewell.
Mark felt unease. With tears he held
His sister as she turned to leave;
And even while the king must grieve,
She was some hours now with child.

7

The ship sailed on accompanied by
The arcs of dolphins following,
Diving and plunging, revelling
In being with them on the sea.
So might Poseidon once have come
In festive dolphins' company
Wreathed by them swimming at his side,
Or Thetis, silver in the tide
With dolphins, promising to give
To Peleus their boundless power.
As Blanchefleur watched them from the deck,
With humorous skill these dolphins played
Not telling who they once had been.
Had one of them saved Ino, then
Reached Corinth with her on its back?
Were they Tyrrhenian pirates once
Who, changed to dolphins when they held
The immortal Dionysus child,
Have dived and surfaced ever since?
Or were they Triton in the foam?
They leaped and paused beside her. – *Look,*
They smiled (then disappeared). *We have
Been everyone who ever lived.
We welcome you, white ocean flower,
And you ill-fated Rivalen.*

8

Dropped anchor, eddying calm, the wash,
Dark gathered oaks, the running marsh;
All Lyonesse honouring this day,
The harbour welcomed them with joy.

They lingered on the narrow bridge
Which, veering at the cliff's long ledge
Crossed a ravine. Here they stood
And looked towards a shallow wood
Which gently sloped towards the sea.
As they walked on, a white stemmed tree
Kept pace with them across the void;
They saw spring branches still in bud
And caught the glittering, glistening lace
Of streams half hidden in the gorse;
They smelt the fields of lavender
And at their feet saw heartsease grow.
That such a world of sweetness should
Not pass! And yet Duke Morgan strode
Outside the gates of Lyonesse
Intent to seize their happiness,
The embodiment of their destiny.
So Rivalen in sorrow leaves
With loyal Rohalt all his loves,
His Blanchefleur and their son to be,
And goes to fight his enemy.

9

Just as Penelope had known
Long years at her unproductive loom
So Blanchefleur at the loom of days
Worked with a weft of fruitless rays
(That light not borne from him), the warp
Her patience waiting without hope.
Of all the forms regaled by light
Unfolding, visiting her room
Not one conformed to Rivalen.
She did not see his face again.

And only those in battle's heat,
To life indifferent, with sword
Upraised, or conscientious blade,
Or undiscriminating pike,
Encountered without seeing him.
For neither death by drowning sea
Nor suffocating earth, nor fire –
None of the elements she knew
Embraced him, but base treachery,
An ambush of a hundred men
Cut down the father of her son.

10

Grief like the smoke beside a field
Persisting, gathering in the air,
Persisted, spiralling in her.
She spoke to no one, shed no tear.
When Rohalt briefly thought her healed,
And hoped to coax her back to court,
She said – *I have no other thought*
Than to be finished with this world.
Grief like the smoke beside a field
Which sleeps all day until, at night,
It finds fresh fuel and flourishes,
      Fanned out, unfurled in her.
Unfurled in her, her son stirred;
In lonely grief she gave him birth.
She wept, she wet him with her tears
She smiled to see his sighing breath
And then she spoke to him – *Fair child,*
The fairest child born to this world,
Born now in sadness shall be called
      Tristan. And so she died.

11

Tristan is named in sadness. Time
Moves through the slow constricting glass.
And yet his birth is favoured by
Illustrious visitors. The sky
At dawn depicts a chariot
Of saffron cloud suffused with light.
Nature disdaining melancholy,
Cupid with a single dart
Appears, steps down on cloud steps, from
His tiny coach of atmosphere.
Resplendent on a shimmering stair,
Posed with pilasters of peach air
He laughs. He will not ever share
In grief. He likes to play.
Indulgently his mother smiles,
For, in the absence of the gods
Of Lyonesse or Cornwall, all
Still occupied with funeral
Orations, those for Rivalen
And Blanchefleur's now blanched flower, the bier
Beneath the oak which shades the sea,
Comes Cupid with a Roman sky,
One coloured by Vesuvius'
Rose turbulence, flesh limning veils.
And Venus stands against the sun
Whose rays affect a jewelled crown
Of emanations from her hair.
While Tristan sleeps, still unaware,
She scatters roses recklessly,
All gathered from the curling clouds
Like some marine anemone,
      Across the sleeping boy.

12

We now pass over Tristan's youth
Or, at the very least, accelerate
Through early years, their rapid growth
Both physical and spiritual,
Until the world bathes in his light,
For all know well the tedium
Of dutiful accounts, well meant,
Of aptitude at numbers, skill
With harp and lute as well as sword,
Of muscular development,
Prodigious feats bending the bow,
The growth of virtue, noble brow,
Precocity, outstanding charm
Et cetera, et cetera.
Suffice to say that Gorvenal
(Who follows Tristan faithfully
Through all his life, on land and sea),
Entrusted with the growing lad
      Soon taught him all he knew.

13

So, fifteen years have passed. The man,
Tristan, now contemplates a plain.
Its bounds are hills voluptuous
Which cast long shadows like the trace
Left following vessels on the sea
Long after they have passed. Now see,
Where milk-white or pale violet light
Announces uncontained delight,
His destiny prefigured: now,
The plain is rich as tasselled grain;
A woman moves towards Tristan
As if she travelled in the prow
Of an invisible ship. He pales.

Mysterious she sighs and smiles
Resembling that fair Venus who
Attended, with her son, his birth
(Perhaps with inappropriate mirth),
Her hair as radiant as her face,
The sun confused within that grove.
She sets him firmly on a path
      Which he will never leave.

14

Norwegian sailors now intrude,
The next of many instruments
Of fate which, like a writhing beast
Or goaded dragon breathing fire
Scorching the woods on every side,
Will take fair Tristan from his course.
With Nordic lore they lured him first,
Then seized him. But, to give due praise,
Tristan resisted them for hours;
The sun was high above the mast
Before they had him safely tied,
So great, so admirably immense
Was Tristan's valour. And in this
They knew they held a worthy prize.

15

Until, that is, morality
Which stirs below the sentient sea
(Or so say ancient mariners)
Observed that turbulence and rose;
The ocean will not countenance,
For long, rapine or felony
And in its slow, majestic dance
Saw, in that hull, injustice rule.

While slow to rouse, once roused, it will
Leave no stone in its path unturned.
It hunched its shoulders, freed its hands,
Like some great beast which bathes then stands,
White water streaming from its flanks
(While distant waves assail its banks).
It tossed the ship from hand to hand,
The ship was hurled and handled here
So roughly that all Norway cried,
– *The storm which drives us from our course*
These birds, these dark, wet cliffs, their sluice
Which will engulf us all – for fear,
This boy has put a curse on us.
Cast him adrift, get rid of him
And let us sail again in calm.
They thrust him off in a small boat;
Both wind and raging sea abate.
Then, swiftly on a mirrored cloud,
And idling with the tide, he sees
Base Norway dwindle and recede,
And next, a citron beach and trees;
Then calm waves cast him safe ashore.

16

Intransigent the distance seemed.
A grey salt forest lined the shore.
Of such a place had Adam dreamed
When, savouring the apple's core,
He felt expulsion imminent?
Perhaps great Ovid, cruelly sent
To exile, saw the prospect thus,
A solitary barren place
With alien trees crowding the land.

One tree which put down staining fruit
And brittle bright stellated leaves
Attracted Tristan. There he stood
As, everywhere in that great wood,
Paths seemed to lead to clustered groves
Each one intent on seizing light
As candles glow beneath the hand.
Just then, as darkness moved to fall,
A stag burst from the woods. Alert,
Startled, it paused at Tristan's feet.
And then the hounds burst through the brush
With hunters following. But here,
We leave out much which others tell
About the art of venery
And, having killed the stag, the skill
The venesector's art requires,
And other scientific lore
Concerning venison. In short,
Tristan was greeted royally
And offered all that he might wish
As solace for his bitter sighs,
And welcomed back with them to court.
    The place was Tintagel.

17

The castle shone within its wall.
Surrounding orchards sang in rows
With groves of trees in antiphon;
Streams rich in fish divided these;
Ploughed lands and gardens stood between.
The whole seemed like a game of chess
Whose king was unassailable.

To Tristan all seemed happiness
And yet some further element,
      A strange presentiment,
Was present often. Often too,
(Such speculation is not new)
Fortune seemed here more changeable
As if a balance were set free
And every possibility
Encouraged. Then might knight or pawn
Move everywhere without constraint.
He sensed that freedom in the sea
Which, studying him, seemed limitless.

                ❧

18

King Mark looked up and saw Tristan.
A cloth depicted, on the wall
Behind him in the smoke-filled hall
Events which he had often seen
But which seemed puzzling now. He said
– *Tristan, some echo in your face*
Affects me, yet I cannot place
The likeness. And then he sighed
Remembering Blanchefleur of his blood.

                ❧

19

King Mark called Dinas of Lidan,
His seneschal – *Something there is*
About the youth which troubles me,
Some echo, or a joyful dread
To which Dinas replied – *My lord,*
His knowledge of that venery
Our hunters marvelled at, his wise
Discoursing, his great courtesy...
Who is this sadly named Tristan?

20

King Mark looked up and said – *Tristan,*
Some echo in your face affects
Me strangely. But no more of this.
A singer out of Wales has come
Whose reputation reaches us
At court before him. Listen well.
The harpist now began to play
And filled the hall with melody.
At once, Tristan, at his first notes,
Cried out – *This is an ancient song,*
Derived from Brittany, and known to me.
It celebrates an ancient love.
Note how the melody inflects
And turns upon itself. It needs
The touching skill we're told you have.
The Welshman did not speak, but played.
The subtle melody indeed
Did turn upon itself, and trail
And twist into a kind of braid,
Whose long entanglement his skill
Disintricated for their ears.
And then he said – *What would a boy*
Like you of tender swaddling years,
Know of the skills required to play
Such melodies? Here, give us deeds,
Not words. And Tristan took the harp
And played the same strange melody.
He made it turn and cross and trace
Its own reflection in a pool;
He made it like an interlace
In granite softened by the wind
Which on our crosses still we see.
His touch was delicate yet strong,
The final circling cadence long.

And from that company a cry went up
When all this shimmering reached an end.

21

The harpist said – *Youth, you play well*
Of that we're sure. But can you play
With one hand tied behind your back
And harmonise in parallel?
Then Tristan leaning at the oak
Said, with the traces of a smile,
– *Harpist if you but whistle it*
I'll see if I can follow you.

22

King Mark was silent, wondering.
Dinas said – *Wonderful! Sir king,*
This youth was meant to reach us here.
He must stay with us this long year
And longer. Mark then spoke:
– *Tristan you stand within that oak.*
Its leaves could not outnumber all
Your skills and virtues. Tintagel
Now begs you: stay this year with us.
And Tristan answered. – *Some great force*
Determined that we meet. Its seas
Transported me to these salt shores.
We cannot overrule its hour
Nor ever question its great power.
Whatever you would have me do
I'll gladly do for you, and stay.

23

Events to come were fashioning
Already such affection as
Bound Mark and Tristan. Every day
They rode together to the fields
Or knelt at service; more and more,
Mark trusted Tristan with his heart
And spoke of matters of the court.
And, if the king were sad, Tristan
Would improvise, some way apart,
On ancient melodies. The door
To King Mark's chamber yields
To Tristan gladly now. The way
Through all the court he takes with ease,
As to their hearts in everything.

24

For three long years while Tintagel
Embraced in love its visitor,
Rohalt had sailed in search of him.
At length across that length of sea
(In all our narrative so far
Already several times traversed),
Rohalt embarked and soon, by chance,
(If by this word we mean the power
Of wisdom after the event)
Reached Cornwall's shore.
        And, what is more,
He soon reached Tintagel and went
Directly to the king – *This flower
I bring from Lyonesse. A trance
Has lain on us since we were worsed
By Morgan in a bitter war
To end which, irrevocably,*

I show you this undying flame,
The ruby once held by Blanchefleur
Whose son, Tristan, stands in your hall.

25

King Mark saw Rohalt and the sun
Together climb the cliff's slow side.
He saw a stranger in his court
And welcomed him as was his due.
He saw the banquet through a dew,
Saw float before him crimson caught,
That ruby for which Blanchefleur sighed,
And Tristan now his sister's son.

26

As soon as this great startlement
Had been resolved and spread abroad,
And praise and happiness declared
The king armed Tristan as a knight
And made him ready to return
Once more across the dangerous sea
To end Duke Morgan's tyranny
In Lyonesse. Then, at dawn,
When in the harbour King Mark's fleet
Stood waiting, everything prepared,
Tristan boarded. Tears were shed
That lesser men could not be sent.

27

To leave in tears at last
A pastoral world of sheaves in fields,
Folds of hills where foxglove glowed,

Flood-plains rich in curling grasses,
Horses waiting these to grow,
Snow drifts, castles set on hills,
Rills, embankments, shadowed groves,
Rivulets with moss in islands
Hands of hanging fruit in trees,
Breezes fanning eager faces,
Traces of a path through leaves,
   To leave and lose all this!

     ❧

28
And after many days and nights
And many days and nights of long
Protracted weary skirmishing,
Fixed battles, sieges, brandishing,
Masked knight encountering masked knight,
Uncertain meetings in the woods,
Dark work with earthworks, clarion calls,
Horrendous hackings, broken blades,
Swords crossed and severed in a blow,
Brave Tristan slew Duke Morgan.
       Then
He spoke thus – *Now that Lyonesse*
Is given back to peace, I face
This conflict of the heart: Rohalt
Who gave me all my youth and Mark
To whom I owe this victory
And all the ties of lineage –
Both have great claims on me. My lords,
The free man has two things: the land,
Which he must fight to free; and, next,
His body. These he freely gives
In service to his lords. For me,
(And, men who bravely served me well
And are in need of sustenance,

*I will be brief), Rohalt must take
And govern here this fragrant land,
(Which now I gather in my hand)
While I return to Tintagel
      And loving serve King Mark.*

Part Two

29

A multiplicity of airs
Beguiled the banquet table as
At every quarter minstrels played
To celebrate Tristan's great deed,
And his return. In triumph crowned,
He floated in this sea of sound,
Rejoicing, at his uncle's side,
Until a shadow crossed the ground.
A multiplicity of airs
Were vented from the Irish sea
And, blown from every quarter, fanned
The court and all that company
Who celebrate Tristan returned,
In triumph crowned. Then messengers
Announced – *Morholt has come.*
The breeze had stirred the banner, hung
Behind the king, its billowing
Disturbing its heroic scene,
Its figure pleated, narrowing.
The messenger announced – *My king,
Alas, base Morholt has been seen.*

30

Two minstrels to the court propose:
– *A riddle: What distinguishes
The whale which swallowed Jonah whole,
Fearsome and vast, with giant bones,
And Morholt standing on a hill
About to swallow Cornwall. Well?
The answer, lords and ladies, will,
I venture not surprise you: One
Wears ragged clothes and hides his loins.*

*— Another riddle: What is huge
And horrible and has more hands
Than all the monsters in these lands?
The answer: Morholt in a rage
About to seize our Cornish dues.
— Another riddle: What would we
Most in this dark world wish to see?
The answer: Morholt's shadow flee
And Morholt die beneath the sea.*

31

Morholt the Mountain from the North
Morholt the Mouth, the Drouth of Mirth,
The Knight of Frightening Height and Girth,
Morholt, Collector of those dues
Which Cornwall owed to Ireland by
Some ancient statutes, not repealed,
Cruel Morholt, the Enforcer, spoke:
*— Good king we do not wish to wield
Our power over Cornwall. You
Have only to supply our need
Which ancient treaties have decreed:
Three hundred pounds of copper first;
We got that without laying waste,
And then of silver, then of tin.
And now, this year, your able Youth:
Three hundred youths and maidens drawn
By lot from all of Cornwall, then
To serve in Ireland's misty green.
As usual, the offer stands,
If any knight with his own hands
Should care to fight with me alone
He could for all his kinsmen win
The forfeit of this treaty. Well!
Is anywhere there such a knight?*

32

Morholt was huge (as we have said)
But, once more, we elaborate:
Like shadows in the peat-moss bog,
His face was dark and vast. He glared,
His chest a trunk, each arm a log;
The massive neck which bore his head
Was fearsome. So were his arms and thighs.
To stress again his fearful size:
He towered over every knight
Ranged round the sombre festive board,
The way the Easter moon appears,
Which rises vastly (as did Our Lord)
And fills the sky above the sward
Seeming the larger for the fringe
Of elms and oaks which darkly range
Below the crest and stand against
Its eminence. Just so, Morholt
Commanded all the seated court.
Or picture how a valley will
When first one climbs its vantage hill
Seem larger still seen from that height.
Morholt was massive (there is no doubt,
As has been clearly pointed out).
The barons fumed in helpless rage
   But none took up the gage.

33

Three times the challenge was thrown down,
Three times those knights seemed lost for words,
All fallen silent like small birds
Caged with a hawk. So, Morholt cried,
– Well then, my lords. Let us proceed
To the drawing of lots, that I may take

Your children to my king. Tristan
Spoke then to Mark – *My liege, you know
The love I bear for you and so
For Cornwall. Therefore let me go
To fight Morholt.* King Mark was slow
To rise and answer; dark his frown,
As Tristan waited and the lake
Of knights around him waited. Now
The king could see that nothing would
Restrain the son of Blanchefleur's blood
      But Morholt's fearful sword.

34

The scattering of crocuses
So strangely leafless in the snow,
The mottled window of the room,
Where seneschal and servants came
To arm him heavily (for we know
Already of Morholt's great size),
The tree which stains the ground below
With seeds of crimson spilling fruit
Where once he drifted to the coast,
The castle in a morning mist,
Soft lightning in the woman's eyes
Who brought and poured the bowls of mead,
A humid star high in the west,
A dark and unconfiding moon –
Something had blurred the difference
Between his mingled memories
And real events accompanying him
Along the path to Morholt's sword.
Heavy with arms, weighed down in fears,
He stepped into the morning sun.

35

A scattering of crocuses,
The bright bells pealed across the land,
The dewscape waking to their sound;
But, waking to this morning's fears,
The solemn bells no longer pealed
But loudly tolled. Tristan with Mark
Emerged across the breaking frost.
The mottled sky a tree-lined shape,
The castle in the morning mist,
The moon remote through rising cloud,
Tristan heard just a single bell.
Conducted to the waiting boat
Tristan was cold. Fearful, remote,
Tristan in armour could not tell,
Of signs that washed across the crowd
Of people standing at the strand,
Which were the present, which the past.
The barons huddled there, aghast,
Ashamed, yet nourished fragile hope
Like seedlings struggling in cold ground.
The boat pushed off, into the sound.

36

The island of St Samson, where
The two contenders were to meet
And fight, was sandy, dank and wet.
Decaying leaves perfumed the air.
The trees hung down like dark, slashed hair.
Tristan waited. Morholt had raised
A purple sail which praised the light
As, billowing, it brought his boat
Towards the rippling sand. He eased
The rudder, turning at the shore,

And then with jeering cries leaped out
And made the eddying hull secure.
But Tristan pushed his with his foot
To float away from shore. Morholt
Shouted – *Fool! Why did you do that?*
And Tristan smiled and said – *Good Sir,*
    In just a little while
But one will need your purple sail.

37

No man must see them fight. And yet,
Three times the salt breeze seemed to bring
The sounds of their contention, or
The ring of sword on sword. At noon,
A purple sail appeared, as bright
As birds which preen but do not sing.
The purple drifted in to shore
And, as all Cornwall feared to learn
What seemed already all too clear,
A wave lifted the vessel near,
And in the prow brave Tristan stood,
In each raised hand a crimson sword.

38

Wild cries of joy. Boats surged out. Boys
Swam out to sea to see Tristan,
Tristan triumphant in the prow,
The sky in tangled braids of light
All turning back to welcome him,
The radiant figure of King Mark.
In this clerestory of rays
He spoke – *Who mourn slain Morholt, praise*
His valour. See the force required

To overcome him: from this blade
A shard has shattered, so great the blow
Morholt demanded for his ease.
Mourners of Ireland, take his frame
And grant him Ireland's tussocked calm.
And keep the shard, in Cornwall made,
Now lodged in this empty lifeless frame,
As tribute. But to my own king
My joy and purpose, let me speak.

39

The King of Ireland's sister fell
And mourned Morholt, her husband, dead
At Tristan's hand. Fair as their land,
The King of Ireland's daughter was
Iseut the Fair.
                          Let all stand still,
Let wooded hills, moist cliffs of shale,
The perfumed copse, the glimmering rill,
The skies' recumbent clouds, the vale –
Let all of these in homage pale
At Iseut's naming in the tale,
Who, fairer than the faintest sail
On evening's darkening ocean swell,
                  Now vowed to hate Tristan.
Tristan of Lyonesse she vowed
            To seek until his death.
She and her mother often had
By unguents, herbs and remedies
Healed mortal wounds. But here
Morholt lay dead. Iseut drew out
The shard of steel (from Tristan's sword)
And kept it in a phial. She cried
– Tristan of Lyonesse, beware.

40

King Mark led Tristan through the field.
King Mark led Tristan, wounded foal.
King Mark led. Tristan, wounded, fell
Into Mark's arms. He had not felt
In all the time since Morholt failed
And stumbled, pain he could not foil.
And when this wound had still not healed
He bathed it at the river's shoal
And lay beneath the tolling bell
In beating pain, and wrapped a pelt
Of unicorn where dark, impaled,
His thigh still bled its wine-dark oil.

❧

41

His wound would lead him to Iseut.

The stench of pain had grown so great
Which Mark, nor his doctors, could not staunch,
He asked to be set adrift, once more,
An open boat to be his fate
As once before he'd drifted out
To fortunate isles. Again he'd let
The ragged tassle of events
Unravelling across the sea
Determine how his wound might mend.

A thread would lead him to Iseut.

❧

42

King Mark and Dinas, seneschal,
At length persuaded, saw him glide
Alone, as he had begged to do,

Into the open sea. They knew
That without rudder, oar or sword
He must in fortune vest all hope.

He asked only to have his harp;
All but their love he cast aside,
Content at length to drift aground.

He lay, so wasted by his wound,
The harp's faint echo by his side,
That all he saw were sun and star.

At last some fishermen, feathering oars
Near Whitehaven, on the water heard
A plaintive tune, note by slow note.

A stranger in a drifting boat
With mortal wound was softly rowed
To waiting Iseut's castle wall.

43

Delirious for seven days,
He saw the sky as from a well.
The sea welled up and wrote its name
      Across the drifting keel,
      Volume or *What You Will.*
But soon a second wave welled up,
Effaced the first and wrote in foam
      Along the juddering hull,
The sea's a tangled skein of wool;
One thread will lead you where it will
Until Whitehaven fishermen
Heard music float along the swell.

44

The stranger whom Iseut embraced
With all her healing heart and skill
Was he whom she had vowed to kill
Avenging Morholt's death. A blade
From that knight's armoury had pierced
And poisoned through his thigh the blood
Of Tristan, stranger to her still.
No one who might have known his face
Now saw him. And the poison's toll
Had made him hardly that Tristan
Whom she must spurn. The slightest trace
Of that life fluttered faintly in
His veins. Unconscious, scarce alive,
He dreamt an endless narrative,
In which the sea became a vast
Repository of memory
Which carried him towards some coast,
But would not wet his trailing glove.

45

At last, slowly and painfully
Tristan of Lyonesse returned
To be again that form, which sea,
Her philtres and her loving care
Restored, who should by her be spurned.
He breathed a strangeness in the air.
He asked his fair-haired captor – *Where
Am I, who scarcely know my name?*

46

And when she told him that he lay
In Ireland's verdant lap, not far

From buried Morholt, he began
To improvise a tale, for fear,
      He said – *My name is Tantris.*
Most gently lady, I have been
A seer, one who may sometimes know
The future. Travelling on a ship
To Spain to learn the complex art
Of divination by the stars
Perfected by the Moors of late
With convoluted algebra,
We suffered shipwreck. Pirates then
Seized us as slaves and all our goods
And, were it not for sudden storm,
Which caused in them such great alarm,
I may have never known these glades.
They cast us, each in an open boat,
      Into the unknown seas.
Recovered now, his only thought
Was that he was again that one
Whom Morholt's knights might recognise
And, therefore, that he must escape.
Thus, after many strange events,
Adventures, marvels, accidents,
Which led him out of Ireland's shades
He found himself safely again
      At marvelling King Mark's side.

Part Three

47

In those days, Mark ruled troubled lands.
Dissent was sown. For their own ends,
By whispered rumours, calumny,
Four barons watered its dry seeds.
One of these knights was Ganelon.
(His namesake in another tale
Betrayed and plotted Roland's fall
To bring himself to Charlemagne.)
And now these barons cast their shades
Across King Mark and Tristan's joy
At his return, restored to life.
They spread the rumour that the king
(And this perhaps contained some truth)
Refused to marry lest his wife
Produce an heir to thwart the line
Which must take Tristan to the throne.
In murmurings against that youth
      Dark Ganelon spoke:
– Who is this Tristan? How do we know
What he intended, coming here?
And is he not a sorcerer
Or warlock? Look. Consider how
He beats the Morholt. Next we find
He overcomes a mortal wound
By floating in an oarless boat
For weeks and weeks. It's sorcery!
And look at how he sways King Mark.
That harp accompanies everything.
The sorcerer who would be king!

48

The barons were convinced by dark
And devious Ganelon. At last
There were such clamourings that Mark
Agreed, but on his terms: he would
Give thought to who might be his bride,
One worthy of great Cornwall's pride,
One who might heal the fractious past,
One most deserving of their praise –
And tell the knights in forty days.

49

The morning of the fortieth day
Dawned bright with rising mist, a fierce
But hidden sun above the leaves.
It moved to melt the bearded ice
On trees framed in his window. Groves
Awoke with birds loudly at play
Without a word about his quest.
He still lacked all resolving thought,
Until a strange solution came:
Two swallows, swerving, veering past
Turned back and flew into the room
Locked in affectionate dispute.
Then circling high, as if they sought
A second window opposite
They left. And in the silver air
There slowly fell a golden hair,
A single thread of ductile gold,
So bright it seemed this thread had brought
The sun indoors. He called his knights
And said – *My lords, be now consoled.*
I will do as you wish. But you
Must seek and find her whom I choose.

They clamoured still – *And who is that?*
Here Mark held up the thread of gold
And said – *Why, she whose hair this is.*
The knights, seeing themselves reviled,
Now turned on Tristan thinking this
Some sign of his complicity
Or even greater sorcery,
But he said – *Sirs, may it bring us bliss,*
I recognise this thread of gold
And know its source, and undertake
For King Mark and for honour's sake
To find this bride and bring her back.

50

Once more the sea is bearing him,
Directing him towards its calm
Whitehaven harbour, once the home
Of Morholt, now his grave. A storm
Deflects their ship's course. In alarm
The helmsman struggles. But the arm
Of ocean lifts the ship from harm
And carries it towards that dome
Which dominates the port. A palm
(So strangely like a hand, its name
Perplexes him a second time),
Stands proudly at the harbour's rim.
Encountering the running stream
Which flows through verdant Irish loam
To nudge their hull, they turn in foam,
Then anchor. Now they must assume
The role of merchants, and must seem
Companions of healed Tantris, come
In gratitude to Ireland. Gloom
Of nightfall follows them. The flame
Of candles lights an Irish bloom:

He sees her like a waking dream,
Iseut advancing through the room,
      Her hair a golden plume.

51

Soon after dawn they heard a grim
And dreadful cry. It came
From somewhere near the city wall.
Tristan shuddered. He felt a yeast
Ferment his blood, so dark the sound,
So fearful and inhuman, so
Unlike the cry of any beast,
So agonised, so low yet shrill,
As if a chasm had split the ground
And devils cried in fire below.
And then a silence fell, but one
In which the sound will soon resume.
A woman, frightened, looking down,
Her cloak held at her face, in haste
Explained to Tristan – *Sir, it is
The dragon of the city gates.
No man may pass and take his ease
Outside these walls, until a girl,
An innocent from Ireland's shores,
Is brought to it. But that's not all –
It's horrible. I saw it once!
It seizes her with fiery claws
And then, good Sir, and then, it eats.
For virgins here there's no defence.
The king has offered a reward:
Whoever brings him proof the beast
Lies dead against the smouldering sward
Will win Iseut, his daughter's hand.
But no one's won. And understand*

This, Sir. While we stand talking here
        The beast is very near!
Still Tristan held her back. He cried:
– *One further question. Tell me: Could*
A man of woman born prevail
Against this dragon? Then that wail,
Bloodthirsty and importunate
Which made their veins freeze into ice
Thickened the air again. She stared,
Wide-eyed with fear. She said:
– *He might, I think, if he believed*
Sufficiently in destiny
And could foresee his future, bright
        And strange and marvellous.

52

Dismayed, and yet strangely at ease,
Tristan thought only of Iseut
And how, this way, he might win her
For Mark. For Mark was in his thought
Always. He sojourned here for him;
He crossed strange lands and tutelary seas
For him; he thought of him with calm.
And everywhere he went, he bore
The hopes of Cornwall high, and wore
The swallows' thread close to his heart.

53

For Mark he armed himself and left
At dawn. He galloped from the quay
With armour and regalia
And horse he'd hidden in the hold,

Across Whitehaven's echoing frost
And rising fingers of white mist,
Brightly bold, to meet the dragon.
Towards him raced five horsemen. One
Who veered towards him as they passed
He almost plucked from his saddle by
His long red braided hair. – *Where,*
Cried Tristan – *is the dragon's lair?*
The other's voice which faded fast
Cried out a warning. But Tristan
Urged on his horse towards the east.

54

The dew of his resolve shone bright
On fields and branching roads he passed,
Not ever slowing lest it might
Evaporate with morning's light.
The sights and sounds were brilliant. Birds
Were flittering still in dark fledged trees,
A flowering branch seemed half dissolved
In its own nectar, junipers
Divided and diverged in peaks,
As he climbed rapidly towards
The Country of the Pinnacles.
A vacant sky above the hills
Implied that here were poisoned clouds
Through which no birds would ever fly.
All waited for the rising sun.
His horse was tired. As they slowed
He pondered dragons. Were they real
Or merely agencies of all we fear?
And so, did Perseus slay truth?
Can dragons spring from dragons' teeth?

Was Cadmus then so prodigal
That dragons' teeth have fallen here
So far from sunlit Thebes? Or were
They carried here by violent storms
And in this strange volcanic soil
Have grown into his adversary?
And might he soothe this dragon's fire
By playing sadly on his harp
As Orpheus with his lute had done?
The faint, indifferent, fading moon
Made him think not. A distant roar,
As chilling as it was before,
Changed doubt into familiar fear,
And Tristan felt his quarry near.

55

He reined his tired horse and stared:
The galleries of rock declared
The Country of the Pinnacles.
Stone lay on stone, and on each cliff,
Chimneys of stone capped every peak
As if this crater were the work
Of some slow coral mountain. Bleak
And windswept turrets, corridors
And ramparts made the place a maze
Where no path leads to others. Trees
Were wayward, tangled and distraught.
A copper beech stood full in leaf
Which scarcely spoke of autumn yet,
Despite the desolation there.
A thorn bush gestured at the bluff.
A constant wash of shadows, air,
Which tirelessly flowed back and forth,

Turned leaves to silver in the heath
And gorse. His horse, wanting to graze,
Took several steps. Then, as he feared,
The cliffs rang out; the beast appeared.

56

Dissimilarity combined
From head to tail, from part to part,
To make the dragon horrible.
The dragon is a composite,
And thus most frightening, because
All multiplicity we find
Perplexing. Tristan's horse reared up,
Its hackles raised, its nostrils flared.
Clearly the strumming of a harp
Would not help here. Tristan saw this.
He studied now this multiple:
The head a snarling crocodile,
A lion's paws, a serpent's tail
The body of a griffin, wings
All tipped with scale like shooting stars.
All this Tristan could recognise.
And yet its baleful gazing made
His fear half melancholy. Still
He drew his sword and drove his horse
Towards this dark ophidian side
While over it an awkward wing,
Itself equipped with claws, might bring
Disaster. Fiercely he struck, but all
His strength could still not hurt that hide.
The creature felt the blow. It clawed
And seized his shield. He struck again,
His breast unshielded, but in vain.

And next, the vitriolic flame
From smoking nostrils seared the name
Emblazoned on his helm. He paled.
His horse fell down. He paused. He reeled.
But bravely, as the phoenix sings
Amidst the flames, he plunged his sword
Down through the throat and pierced the heart.
The creature gazed and slowly fell.

57

He took the dragon's tongue, as proof,
And hid it in his clothes. But soon
That acrid blood against his skin
Had poisoned him and, in a swoon,
He fell amongst the mounds of turf.

The seneschal, Guerrain The Red,
Who, fleeing from the dragon's lair
Had pointed Tristan galloping there,
Returned. He smelt the smouldering air
And found the creature, staring, dead.

He took its head (now safely slain)
And hastened to the king's assize
To claim Iseut the Fair, the prize
He long had coveted. Desires
Impel deception, and Guerrain

Pretended to have killed the beast,
And showed its head to all the court.
The king was startled but could not doubt
Such evidence. And so he brought
Iseut the Fair to meet at last

Her husband. She was sceptical.
This coward could not kill a hare.
And so she took her maid and squire,
Brangain and Perinis, to where
Guerrain had claimed such fearless skill.

They found the road, and there a trail
Not made by Irish hooves. They found
The dragon dead, and on a mound
The shield's scorched arms on blackened ground,
And there too, Tristan, breathing still.

58

And Tristan, breathing still, they brought
        In secret to the court
And in the women's rooms undressed
And bathed him (he who was so young)
And found the poisoning dragon's tongue
And knew that he and not Guerrain
        Had there the dragon slain.
The queen spoke on Iseut's behalf:
— *Our seneschal must prove the serf*
We know. And you, with two days' rest,
Shall challenge him upon the field
And tell his lie to all the world
And prove him false.
        Tristan was weak,
But for Iseut the Fair's fair sake
He willingly agreed. And so the queen
Made healing potions of that green
Which burgeons over Ireland. Then,
Tristan at times forgot King Mark.

59

The following morning, as he woke,
As sunlight teased each gilded ray
Across the shoulders of the day,
Iseut prepared a healing bath
Of warm and scented water. Oil
And herbs and strangely perfumed balm
She added with her mother's skill,
Then helped him from his curtained bed.
She looked at him and he at her.
She smiled to find him beautiful,
And noted warmly that his youth
And vigour seemed in time restored.
Then Tristan smiled through clouds of steam
To see her dazzling flax of hair
And knew he'd found the Queen of Gold.
But when she saw his lingering smiles
She worried lest she may have failed
In any one of several rules
Which courtesy dictates for guests;
She wondered suddenly: Perhaps she should
Have polished all his arms, his sword?
She went to where his armour lay,
Where sunlight lingered with each ray;
How valorous this knight must be!
His arms suggested noble birth.
And then she drew his sword. In blood
It still bore stains. She brought a cloth
And as she polished it she saw
That it was notched and pitted; more,
A shard had shattered from a blow
And parted from the blade. The gap
Described a curious fateful shape.

She hastened to the phial which hid
The dreadful fragment. Then she cried
A frightful cry. She held the sword
Above her head. A heavy ray
Of clouded sunlight struck the blade.
She held the sword above her head
Advancing, past the empty bed,
To where he revelled in the bath.

60

She held the sword above her head,
And in a startled voice she heard
Her own distraught excited rage
Cry out. – *Tristan!* she cried,
Tristan of Lyonesse, who slew

*My mother's brother on the Isle
Of Samson, staining that purple sail –
Now you are naked here, and weak,
Unweaponed in this perfumed pool,
My resolution must not fail.*

Tristan could not evade the blow
But spoke to save his life – *You know,
Iseut, but do not know. My life
Is yours already: once saved now,
And once as Tantris in your cure.*

*Nor did I blacken Morholt's name.
No treachery has brought me shame,
And, furthermore, consider this:
The seneschal will press his claim
Unless I live to challenge him.*

*Two swallows brought a single hair
To Cornwall. For my uncle there,
I undertook to find and win
Its source, who is Iseut the Fair,
To whom I would allegiance swear.*

She wavered at this argument.
The seneschal and his intent
Must certainly be soon exposed.
And Tristan looked so innocent
As, with the steam, her anger went.

Iseut put down the heavy sword
And in his armour found the thread,
And kissed him gently on the lips,
And clothed him richly. Then she said
– *And is it Mark that I must wed?*

61

The King of Ireland now held court.
A hundred barons sat in state.
The seneschal could scarcely wait
To state his case, and claim Iseut.
The dragon's head still gave off heat.

Tristan arrived with all his men.
They sat around the Irish throne,
Splendid, mysterious, unknown.
The seneschal leaped up again
Describing how he'd fought alone

And killed the dragon – *Here's its head.
The court takes this, and, in its stead,
I take Iseut. What need be said?*
Iseut then rose and cried – *My lord
And king, I ask now to be heard.*

*There is amongst us one who will
Prove false this scheming seneschal.
But you, my father, must repeal
All legacies of our ill will,
All vengeance which on him might fall,*

*Should he prove worthy. Listen, father! He
Alone has slain the monster. He
Has freed us from its tyranny.
My lord, for all our sakes, agree.*
The king was silent, until a sea

Of barons' voices urged him – *Swear!
And let us all in judgement hear
This claimant. Let him now appear.*
Then Tristan rose and faced them. There,
They recognised the murderer

Of Morholt. Tristan spoke above
Their clamourings. – *Ireland, let me prove
That Honour found Morholt his grave;
This dragon's tongue I took, alive,
As Guerrain fled its stony grove.
And so let Ireland no more grieve;
I come to take Iseut in love
To Tintagel, with Mark to live.*

❧

62

The vow held fast; this was the prince
Who brought to them deliverance
From dragon dread. All that was past.
The king and all his court rejoiced.
Iseut, as troubled as the sea
Embraced Tristan ambiguously:

She heard him say – *To take Iseut
In love*, but for another heart!
To travel on the ocean's side
With him, yet as another's bride.

Part Four

63

The braided sea against the prow
At anchor in Whitehaven cove,
        Its idle ebb and flow
All waited for the cry of Now
At which waves break and creatures move.
Meanwhile, indoors, the queen prepared
A distillation of the past,
By which is meant that clamouring growth
        Of creature, plant and stone,
Which patiently the fruitful sun
Changes and charges with its power.
This ancient synthesis of love
She brewed into an elixir.

64

The wave unfolds and, like a hand,
Pours wine across the waiting prow
Still standing idle at the pier.
Its wash draws lace across the land.
The queen decants the elixir
With care. No precious drop is lost.
The flask is sealed and fuming now
With distillations of the past,
The stuff of future tears. Brangain
Says – *Lady, what does it contain?*

65

It holds itself in readiness,
The queen confided in Brangain.
The world waits in this elixir.

I'll tell you some, if not quite all
That it contains, ingredients
Derived from ancient Irish lore
        And known to me alone:
The berry of the juniper,
The lime of certain migrant birds,
The nightjar and the staring owl,
A perfume from the pistil of
The nightshade, mountain strawberry,
Effusion from the musk-deer, thorns
From vigorous autumn-flowering vines,
A bell-shaped bloom found only in
The Country of the Pinnacles,
The juices of the thistle stem
The pomegranate, aniseed,
The salt tear from a mollusc shell,
All this dissolved in beads of dew.

66

Events which float upon that swell
Were waiting to be singled out.
She said to Brangain – *Since you will*
Be always with Iseut I trust
With you this precious concentrate.
But guard it carefully. You must
Protect it from the wilful world
Until the bridal day, unfurled,
Enswathes King Mark and his Iseut.
And then, when they are quite alone
Bring them this flask as nuptial wine.

67

Time gathers to a single crest
Its sadly joyful morning when
A daughter leaves to live in joy.
The queen said – *Go with her, Brangain;*
Soon you must leave our native coast.
And then she warned again,
– *This elixir will guarantee*
Undying love in every part,
The heart and blood and every limb.
And Brangain promised faithfully
To guard the flask until that time
Which must unite Mark and Iseut.

68

The sun is summoned, following
Above the poplars, as Brangain
Is seen to go on board, to turn
And look towards the open sea.
It singles out the harbour wall
Where Tristan stands, outlines and gilds
A flask which cautious Brangain holds,
And floods with gold Iseut's fair hair.
A close observer from the shore
Might note a certain coolness there
As Tristan (with loyal Gorvenal)
Embarks, and finally Iseut
Parts from the queen reluctantly
To travel with him to the king.

69

The vessel driven on, impelled
By lilting breezes, ploughed the waves
And, as the coast of Ireland paled
And disappeared at last in groves
Of mist, still rising from the sea,
Iseut felt all was contrary;
And when Tristan came to the tent
On deck in which she sat, she sent
Him angrily away. Tristan
Her uncle's murderer who took
Her to his uncle's bed! The deck
Awash with waves in heavy seas
Seemed desolate with the sail's sighs
      Which took her to King Mark.

70

And even when the air falls calm
And drifting with a flaccid sail
The ship turns, to the creaking wail
Of stretching boards and knotted ropes
And cormorants drying outstretched capes,
Iseut thinks only of the home
Which she has left forever. All
The rest she spurns – the pleasant sun,
The island rising up at noon,
Base Tristan's courteous concern.

71

Contingency is marshalling
Its powers to mingle right and wrong.

After some days the breeze is charmed
And lured to another latitude
Leaving the ship drifting, becalmed.
An island with its pumice shores
And fronds, and scattered, beckoning trees
Attracts the crew. Iseut is sad.
Almost alone she stays on board.
Pale sunlight lazes on the deck.
A child plays near her dazzling tent.
Iseut alone finds sunlight bleak;
A shadow conjures her King Mark
And sorrows without precedent.

72

Fresh energies to move them on
Were for a little held at bay.
A stain spread on the listless sea
Which promised to persist. The sun
Stood still. The sailors rowed away
Towards the pumice island shore
Where spilling lava once had met
The dragon-quenching sea. Some lay
In sunlight on that ancient foam
Which shelved down to the foamless sea,
While in its calm swell, others swam.
Brangain walked on the rock ledge. But
Iseut remained, almost alone,
Except for one young child, a girl
      Who for affection stayed
And underneath the lifeless sail
Played and sang songs at her side.

73

Into a dark mysterious stream
While still the empty sail was calm
Their lives were drawn. The breezeless warm
Washed faintly, blithely, over them.
While on the lava island lay
Tristan and all the crew, the day,
Which was to focus like a ray
Their future, lay in waiting. They
Saw breezeless stirrings in the sail.
They heard a soaring seabird call.
Someone was standing in the swell
When, on the distant deck, the girl
Came to Iseut and said – *The sun
Is warm. How beautiful on our skin!
My lady, let me be Brangain
And I will bring you cooling wine.*

74

Another sea flows in our veins
An ocean strewn with flotsam, wracks
Of past illusion, sails becalmed,
Dark sails drawn on towards the crest.
Now love's compelling, glittering wine,
That elixir which should be Mark's,
The distillation of the charmed
Which should bind him to Iseut's breast,
A child now carried to Iseut.

75

A sea which bears upon its tide
A history of calamity
Now carried Tristan to her side,

Impulsively, for courtesy,
Returned to speak to her. Iseut
For courtesy must Tristan greet.
She spoke about the long sea stain,
She poured a bowl of cooling wine
Which, drinking, would inflame them both
In thought, in deed, in life, in death.

76

A dark and troubled, swelling sail
Now floated in the freshening breeze.
The crew returned from pleasures as
Iseut and Tristan drained the bowl.
Brangain, once more on board, resumed
Responsibilities. She came
Towards the couple. Sea-swell loomed.
And, on the straining deck, Brangain
Saw the flask empty. With a cry
She hurled that vessel into the sea.
She cried aloud – *Cursed be the day*
That saw my birth. And cursed the sea
Which brought us to this day. Brangain
Walked to the seated couple. She saw
The flask cast to the deck. She cried
– *Cursed be my birth and cursed this day.*
She grasped, she hurled the empty flask
Into the sea. – *Ah, sweet Iseut*
And you, Tristan, have drunk of joy
And pain and suffering this day.
Across the gentle, billowing sea
A vine had spread into his veins
And Tristan felt its tendril lines
Within his conscious blood, the way
A healing wound, tightening and dry,

Like lightning in a summer sky
Advances, spreading wide its net.
Iseut, too, drank and drank again
Of all that had just passed that day.
A nettle on the forest floor
Moved from her ankle to her heart.
A trailing bindweed bound her. Light
Branched through her branching arms.
Conspiratorial, the sea
Appeared as if a beech in leaf,
Its bracts stirred by an autumn breeze,
Stood just below its surface. All
Of this and more, the world enlarged,
The panoply of sea and sky,
Grew in the forest of their blood.
Brangain stood with the empty bowl
And hurled the past into the sea,
That past now useless as a hull
Subverted by this day now passed,
And the endless present in their eyes.
She watched the flowering of the vine,
And saw their gaze unfocusing,
Enlarging, each with each consumed.

77

On deck, a minstrel sang,

The braided sea against the prow,
The wave unfolds and, like a hand,
It holds itself in readiness;
Events which float upon that swell
Time gathers to a single crest.
The sun is summoned, following
The vessel driven on, impelled.

And even when the air falls calm,
Contingency is marshalling
Fresh energies to move them on
Into a dark, mysterious stream.
Another sea flows in our veins,
A sea which bears upon its tide
A dark and troubled, swelling sail.

Part Five

78

The ship ploughed over sheaves of waves.
Iseut addressed Tristan – *My lord,*
And he said – *I am not your lord,*
I am your servant. – *No*, she said
With gentleness. *I said 'My lord'*
For love of you. Brangain had heard.
Each word was like a drop of blood
Which stained the pool of her regard.
She stood beside them. Still she stared.
She understood. Henceforth, she said,
They would be lost to all the wide
World's freedom, movement, air, for dread
And joyful sorrow, theirs the sword
Of bliss on which the martyrs bled.
Tristan spoke softly. Iseut replied,
Whereat he kissed her lips. She led
Him to her billowing tent. Inside,
They saw decreed their watershed.
Instead of drifting with the tide
They gave themselves now to the flood.

79

As sunset with its dragon flames
Suffused the sea and wrote the names
Of Tristan and Iseut in streams,
Which merged, confusing sea and sky,
The ship drove on through turbulent seas
Until at length it reached the shores
Of Tintagel. And King Mark there
Stood waiting, with his retinue,
The bearer of that lustrous hair
Of fine-spun gold. When day was spent
Iseut stepped from her pleated tent.

Pale she appeared, pale as that gold
Which crowned her. Then she held
The rope which held the ship and stepped
Ashore. And Tristan, following, leaped
To the dock and there embraced King Mark.

80

King Mark cried – *Welcome, and our praise*
To my own Tristan for his quest
So bravely carried out, his days
Of pain and suffering when, distressed,
He sought, for my own sake, Iseut.
And to his sailors too my heart,
Who courting danger reached the coast
Of Ireland charting treacherous seas.
The banquet board was glittering, bright
With artifice and rich delight.
The motif of two swallows joined
By threads of gold was everywhere.
Mark came to Iseut and took her hand,
And said – *My queen-to-be, the Fair*
Iseut who like the pastel air
Is everywhere and in our thought,
To honour whom we gather here,
We welcome you to Tintagel.
Iseut looked round this gallery
Of faces like a sliding sea
That floats below a hidden sun.
She saw the world and, there, Tristan.
The motif of two swallows joined
By threads of gold was everywhere.
The cunning of the culiner's art
Depicted them in marzipan,
In fruit-stained breads, in coloured ice,

In sweetmeats shaped to this device,
In all delights and artifice.
The cloths were all embroidered thus.
King Mark was eloquent. Iseut
Looked round the dazzling gallery
And everywhere she met the gaze
Of those who, curious, judged her fair.
A painted swallow on a board
Was so arranged behind her head
That, when she sat, the bird appeared
To pluck in its beak a floating hair.
At this, and when she moved, there broke
The mingled cries of mirth and cheer.
Two jesters dressed as swallows ran
Darting amongst the banqueters,
A rope of gold between them drawn.
Laughing they captured whom they chose
In coils of that gold thread. And one
Entwined the loop round Tristan's throat
Who, imprisoned, gazed at fair Iseut
  And met her frightened eyes.

81

In all the days since first they drank
And, having drunk, saw then the flask
Thrown to the undivulging sea,
  They had not thought to ask
What hour of day or season passed
Like shadows at an outer door.
Whole branches partly leafed they saw
But whether leaves emerged or fell
  They could or would not tell.
Their world of action had become
Deciduous: across its leaves

Each trod to reach the other. So,
Assiduous in secrecy,
They held a world which soon had shrunk
    To a trembling, brimming bowl.

82

The banns were published in the court.
For eighteen days their Tintagel
Became a set of corridors.
A curtained room, an empty hall,
And paths through groves where they might meet.
King Mark was generous and grave,
Content that after these mild days,
And used to Cornwall and its ways,
Iseut could calmly with him live.

83

Iseut spoke to Brangain.
— While you were on that pumice slope
By sunlight and the sea beguiled
You could not know the fateful child
Would bring us, on that listless deck,
That oceanic cup to drain,
To drain us of the world. Now Mark
Will shortly claim me as his bride.
And he alone still harbours hope.
I do not blame you. But, Brangain,
Listen: I must ask you, my maid,
(As maid you still must be to serve)
To do this thing for me, for love
Which takes root in that emptied cup
And sends its vines through me. As I
Must face a thousand obstacles,

(And all of them impossible)
So Mark expects one obstacle
In me which I cannot provide,
Which Tristan in that luminous tent
Dissolved. But you, Brangain,
For recompense must lie for me,
And on my eager nuptial night
Must be, for Mark, my flowering pain.

   Iseut embraced Brangain.
— *When public revelry is done*
And at the bridal bed we lean
You'll linger. And we'll do it thus:
I'll dazzle and delay the hour
And you must ply him still with wine,
As you were asked so long ago
By the queen, my mother, so to do.
Ply him with wine. Then, languorous,
I'll slowly quench the candles. Then
In breathing darkness, until dawn,
   You will take my place.

85

And so, dawn drew its veil aside
And from its arms above its head
The day drew off its white chemise.
And yet Mark woke to find unease
Had risen with this nuptial day.
The town in splendour round him lay.
Walls shone. Garlands were draped on plinths.
Walking on water-hyacinths
Servants sought fresh fowl for the feast.
Brangain asked for the cellars' best
Bright wine. The tables all were laid
With radiant cloths. But fleeting shade
Mark's royal jubilance belied.

And calling Tristan to his side
He talked then, eager to confide
The uncertainty of hope. And yet,
Tristan himself seemed as remote
As if some valley fell between
The present and that sunlit cairn
Where the king and Tristan once had stood.

86

Iseut in white, a white which was
The absence of all colours, not
The flux of their equality,
Approached the room in candle light.
The last carousers gone, a quiet
Fell and spread through all the court.
King Mark approached. The moon was high,
The hour late. Brangain brought wines.
A solemn bell had ceased. The night
Resigned itself to frost. His smile
Was gentle and compassionate,
For Mark felt love for his Iseut
Which struggled in his troubled heart,
Struggled and grew like some young tree
Against the vine which round it twines.
He thought her beautiful in white,
In candle light. Brangain poured wine.
Iseut was reaching up. He saw
A taper flare then flare no more.
The night ran on ahead of him
Or so it seemed. And here, the room
Was almost empty. Fair Brangain
Was leaning perfumed over him
To pour more wine. Why did he feel
That absence of familiar ghosts,

A vacancy mixed with desire?
No Cupids garlanded the air
Self satisfied, cavorting there
To watch this consummation. Nor
Was Aphrodite standing here
In this increasingly shadowy place;
No Juno Cinxia would unlace
The girdle from this bridal dress,
Like fields of snow in dwindling light;
Nor Hymenaeus standing guard
Lest Attic pirates should intrude –
No one would assuage his loneliness.
The candles guttered, sputtered out;
Iseut quenched many. Soon the flame
Brangain should carry from the room
Burnt still, the only light. Iseut
And Brangain gently drew from him
His royal robes. A blur of white
And darkness reigned over the room.

87

Events emerged now on a plain
Through which there ran a deep ravine.
While flowers grew and trees gave shade,
The sun was often lost in cloud.
And yet the ordered groves seemed calm:
The king was tender to Iseut.
The barons, too, were, for a time,
Content on hearing Tristan's name
Or seeing him at Iseut's side,
To override their jealousy;
Iseut was fêted at the court.
No splendour spared, she moved beneath
A patronage of jewellery

A canopy of flowers, cloth
From Hungary and Thessaly
Embroidered with bright leopards, jays,
Eagles and fauns, and all in praise
Of her beneficent presence. Yet
She spent her days in sadness. As
Was customary, Tristan slept near.
Unspoken love bore little fear.
And yet, and yet, her anguished heart
Was anxious, troubled, passionate.
Always she knew that longing, set
Like another life within her own.
And always too, her maid, Brangain,
She who had served her mistress well,
Was by this made more vulnerable,
For she alone was witness to
Deception. She alone had seen
The emptied flask, the excess of wine
By which the king had been deceived.
Brangain alone knew Iseut loved,
And she alone could recognise
Distraction in her mistress' gaze.
This knowledge opened the ravine
      Across their pastoral days.

88

The words for madness and the woods
Were then (when Tristan loved Iseut)
One and the same. And thus the word
Allowed the chroniclers to record
The hermit who has fled the court,
The wild man of the woods, who lives
In overgrown and tangled groves,
Or lovers in their tangled plight,

Those falling into *demesure*,
As being *wood in wood*. The word
Thus speaks for all that is to come:
Iseut now breathes a wilder air.
Her plaited willow canopy
Above her bridal bed, fiercely
Puts out fresh limbs and leaves until
Its forest closes out the sun.
For this is madness too:

                        Brangain

Who served her mistress faithfully
That mistress now sees as a threat
Because of all that she might tell
Of passion, endangering Tristan.
Unreason nourishes such fears,
Though nothing else could give them cause
In Brangain's services. Yet Iseut,
Obsessed, distraught with love, now calls
Two loyal serfs to her, and says
– *Let no one else within these walls*
Hear of these words... And what they hear
Is so inhuman, cruel, severe
That only love which holds death dear,
Only that pulsing elixir,
The smothering tendrils of her fear –
Only such extremities
Could ever justify her words.

89

– *Into the woods convey the maid*
Whom I will send with you. The king
And Tristan hunt today. Avoid
Their glade. Take her far off.
Kill her and bring back evidence.

Bring back her tongue which could
While ever she might live, be my
Undoing. And bring back report
Of her last words. So spoke Iseut
And promised them their freedom. Then
Trembling she called Brangain. Fortune,
As anyone may shortly see,
Will recognise her innocence,
And favour justice over love
Particularly in the woods.
          She said – *My friend, Brangain,*
You see how I am set upon
By sufferings, how I fret and grieve
And freeze and burn, how everything
In me lacks Nature and its balm.
Go to the wild woods; find the reef
Where spring those healing flowers. Calm
My spirits by what plants you find.
And, Brangain, know I send you there,
Into the woods, to end my care.

❧

90

Brangain set out at once. The woods
Passed rapidly on every side,
Like marching soldiers in disarray,
Those closest rapid and intent,
Those further off more leisurely.
The serfs strode on, one just ahead,
The other close behind. She saw
The fragrant plants she needed. She
Said – *Here will do*. But they cried – *No.*
Don't stop. We must go further still.
Sometimes a felled tree lay across
Their tangled path. Layers of shade
Grew heavier. Then, suddenly,

The man ahead turned with his sword
Upraised. She turned. The other too
Was menacing. One said – *Poor girl,*
We've brought you here to kill you. Words
Alone must save her, yet she knew
No reason for this cruelty.
She fell amongst the nettle grass,
The sword against her throat. One man
Said – *If our lady so decreed*
You must have done some wrong. Tell us.
She said – *My friends, I can recall*
One misdeed only, if misdeed
It can be called. On board the ship
From Ireland, each of us had brought
A snow-white shift and, on the sea,
Iseut had damaged hers. I lent
Her mine, that gown of purest white;
She wore it on her wedding night.
And this is my sole wrong. And yet,
If it is her wish that I should die
Tell her I thank her for the hope
That she has always given me.
The serfs drew back, perplexed. This crime,
If crime it were, seemed scarcely harm
Enough for such a punishment.
They bound her to a tree, and found
The tongue of some wild animal
And to the court returned.

91

At court late morning had grown stale.
The shadows, weary of the wall,
Were gathering in the air. Iseut
Was standing where they'd left her. Still
Distracted and distressed, it seemed,

The queen now turned and asked them – *Well?*
You're back, I see. And did she speak?
The serfs looked nervously. One said
– *I'll tell you all she said. She spoke*
Of one misdeed, if that indeed
(She said) could be said to be so,
She said that once with you, on board
A ship, she'd lent you her chemise,
That you'd torn yours. Snow-white she said
It was, and then she said she would
Remember always (that is, until
Her death, of course) your kindnesses.
Iseut cried out in great alarm.
– *You are both murderers. Loyal*
She was, and true. Why bring her harm?
If humankind could but reverse
The tyranny of happening,
Undo events! How could you bring
Her harm? What shall we tell the king
And fair Tristan of this foul deed?
One serf said – *Lady, do you mean*
(Or have I got this whole thing wrong)
That you would wish our deed undone?
In tears Iseut implored him – *Yes.*
You should have seen. You must have known
That all of this was wrong – the flask,
The wine, the woods, Brangain, Tristan,
          The branching overhead!
– *In fact, my Lady, actually*
We didn't know quite what to do
For the best. The girl seemed innocent
And so (we hope you understand)
We didn't quite complete the task.
In fact, we tied her to a tree.
As sun through sudden parting cloud
Iseut saw parting forest boughs.

Again she asked them to explain,
To which they told the tale again
(The which in detail to relate
Would be repetitive). She sent
One serf to bring Brangain to court
While she detained the other, lest
Their tale were mere expedient.
And when the king and Tristan came
To court, and Brangain had returned,
And the serfs to freedom were released,
So great was Iseut's relief and joy
That, for a time, her troubled sky
Seemed clear. And with Brangain alone
That night they mingled many tears.

Part Six

92

A minstrel in the forest sang,
— And now we take a deeper way
Through darker woods. So far, the sea
Has everywhere impelled events
Determining their accidents,
Splashing our faces in its spray,
Entering the blood as elixir —
But now we meet a greater power,
Determinant of destiny,
The swell of human jealousy.
And so we take the deeper way
Through darker woods far from the sea.

93

Through darker woods and darkening streams
Tristan and Mark rode back to court
At dusk after the hunt. *And then*
(As the old books say nine hundred times)
They passed the barons, Ganelon
And Andret (nephew to the king),
And others, equally inclined
To jealousy, who darkly stand
In shadows by the castle wall.
But in the sunlit royal rooms,
Apart from tears, and curiously, on
Brangain's forearm and wrists the burn
Of rope, as if she had been tied,
Mark saw nothing amiss. The weight
Of all that was to come lay still
Invisible in all its loam
Like seeds cast to the forest floor
Or spiders' webs before they're spun;

And, looking out, the king saw still
The barons with a sombre air
Close by the door. As travellers tell
Of Pompeii, near Vesuvius,
Who've seen the forms preserved in ash
Of actors frozen in the act
Of drinking from a vanished bowl,
So these men governed by the harsh
And bitter jealousy of all
And everything, were frozen too
But by a moment's fatal stare
In which envy arrests their hearts.
Accordingly these barons sought
To sow division and discord
Between the king and Tristan. While
No one had yet surprised the queen
In her lover's arms, because Brangain
Had guarded her with daring tact,
No one could fail to see that love
Which, reined in, still strode on with them
And carrying them would surely bring
      Them to destruction.

94

— *Sir King,* said Andret, *we have known*
Disquieting things which loyalty
Compels us to relate. Your queen
Is loved by all, as it should be,
But one man loves her treacherously.
That man, Sir King, is named Tristan.
For Ganelon and I have seen
What you through love may fail to see:
The telling glance, the over-free
Embrace, the signs of intimacy

Which lets the furtive lover warn
His love with faint and subtle sign...
– *Enough!* the king cried. *Speak no more
To me of this. The passing on
Of groundless rumours must demean
The telling more than him or her
Who suffers it. But see: Tristan
Has all my trust. I would prefer
To trust him over all who ran
To hide in cowardly silence when
Fierce Morholt offered honourable pain
To save our Tintagel. Beware
The shame of slander. But be plain:
         What have you heard or seen?*
– We speak only because we care
For Cornwall and the Cornish crown
For whose smirched honour now we fear.
We came to you reluctantly
But you should watch, as well as we.
They took their leave and left the stain
         Of poison in his ear.

☙

95

The urn of flowers from the woods
Stood on the empty banquet board.
Brangain poured water from a flask.
Just as massed flowers seem to be
Profusely reticent, gazing
While always at the point of speech,
Appearing volubly discreet,
Avoiding asseveration, yet
In all their multiplicity,
Always about to mobilise
Should adoration touch the air,

So, in the palace rooms, Tristan
Must seethe with torment in the blood
While all the while he greets the king
      With calm and equipoise,
Seeming content as self-contained
As iris flowers in a field.
The king began to watch Tristan
Despite dismissing Ganelon
And all his claims. Despite his love,
A wound which never would be healed
      Now made the king pretend,
And fear resounded in his words.
Tristan found it more difficult
To touch Iseut, to gaze into
That brimming wine, her searching eyes
(That elixir made visible),
To join their glances on a wire
Like hop vines strung between two poles.
Brangain could sometimes expedite
Their secret meetings, desperate
Since rare, engulfing each in each
Hurling themselves as from a cliff
Which never could be tall enough.
Brangain poured water from a flask.
The king began to watch Tristan.
The stream grew heavy with its silt.
The flowers wilted in their vase.

                ❧

96

Tristan and Mark together went
To hunt beyond the city wall.
But Mark was troubled. Discontent
Now hunted unremittingly.
He watched, and still he did not see

And did not want to see what all
The clustering worlds must surely know:
That nothing stays beyond reproach.
The forest universe proclaimed
In every silent, sentient tree
Some secret truth, self-evident,
But never spoken. There, each glade
Was eager to impress on him
The leaf implicative, the breeze
Didactic, and the slanted bough,
Imperative and pointed. Each
Regaled him with his darkest fears.
The world of creatures shadowed him.
A shower of sparrows in the trees
Protested facts which all must know.
Drawing conclusion from his plight,
Contaminating every thought,
A falcon in its thermal stream,
A black arc on the turning sky,
Mapped out a world of doubt below.
The lengthening day brought no relief.
The insect world teemed nervously
With revelation, all intent
As the dragon-fly which hovered there,
Following Tristan fitfully;
Like Zeno's arrow motionless,
It seemed arrested on the air
And fixed upon its target. Where
Could Mark find calm assurance, now
That all the world this traitor named?
Tristan rode coolly on ahead
Until Mark called him back at last
And said – *Dear sister's son, I have*
To ask you, for our past great love,
To leave our court. Dear son, a grave

*And fearful calumny, the work
Of malcontents threatens to take
Our peace from us. Even to speak
Of it is dangerous. Go now,
Ask nothing more of this. But know
That I will send for you once more.*

97

The expulsion came, with bitter tears.
To leave the Eden of Iseut,
Iseut the Fair whose fair form was
Itself indeed the garden! Yet
With Gorvenal he rode away
And passing the castle garden paused
Beneath the paradise-apple. Fruit
Hung heavy, as abundant as
The two-year apples when they form,
The yellow skin speckled and flecked
With blood-red spots, whose peel
They used to throw on burning coal
To fill the room with fragrance. Now
Their sudden fragrance saddened him,
Remembering too how Iseut's bed
Was perfumed by them. Now they passed
The slender, pendulous warden pear
As green as glass, and faintly streaked,
The medlar with its shadowy clefts,
And, inter-branched densely with it,
The florid pear of Bergamot
Whose juice, perfumed like melons, flows
From the whitest flesh. They left
With heavy heart. But, past the moat
And outer boundaries of the court
Tristan could not go on, that day,

Beyond the nearby town. And here
They lodged and languished. Tristan said
– *My fate is to feel pain. For, at least,*
When Adam left his Paradise
Eve went with him. But, Gorvenal,
My loss of paradise is worse,
And Adam's torment now seems bliss,
Considering that without Iseut,
With neither fleeting touch or sight
I am to live alone.

98

Brangain found Tristan's house.
While Iseut lay beside King Mark
And stared at empty, humid dark
And still by day must hide remorse,

Brangain spoke fiercely with Tristan
Stressing her lady's anguish. He
Must come to her. But where, for fear,
Might they in safety lie? Brangain

Described an orchard, quite remote
Beyond the castle, fenced and closed
With pointed stakes. There, if he pleased,
Iseut would come in fading light.

The place was dense with large, pleached trees
And, at its furthest point, a pine
Stood spreading, tall, somewhat alone.
And round its trunk a stream, in sighs,

Approached, and, slowed to a widening calm,
Entered a shimmering, steady pool,
And then from there ran on until
It passed below Iseut's own room.

Thus every night Tristan should come
Within the picket stakes and cut
Twigs from this pine, and let them float
To where Iseut kept watch downstream.

Then would she come to him by night
Restrained by stealth, there to embrace
Without restraint his form and face.
        Brangain found Tristan's heart.

99

Tristan leaped over stakes as tall
As trees. The last sun shone through cloud.
The mopoke or the whip'o'will
So sadly mournful as a rule
Sounded like joyful clarions, loud
In Tristan's heart. He heard the spill
Of running streams and found the pool.
The tree was dark. In darker shade
The water shone and moonlight showed
Its fleece. He cut mercurial wood
And as the moon emerged let fall
These precious messengers to glide
Through perilous night to love's high hall.

Iseut now walked in fading light;
The sun lay in the forest's arms
And moonlight frayed the gathering night.
These lights combined like merging streams
And at her feet picked out the white
Of fresh cut stems. In haste, night fell.
She ran towards their orchard bed.

100

A dissertation intervenes
On necessary euphemism
And all the strange improbable
Impossibility, in art
Of rendering the generative parts
Of those, like Tristan and Iseut,
For whom they are, by paradox,
The true, the very instrument
Of transportation from the flesh
To visionary Elysiums,
While still contained, constrained on earth.
This is indeed a mystery.
For, on their secret orchard ground,
Iseut and Tristan now pursued
The bliss of interleafing arms
(The way the orchard trees had grown,
Where branches bearing differing fruit
Had interpenetrated here),
Each spirit reaching out to touch
Its physical concomitants,
Each so adoring that it seemed
Each, of the other, now desired
To travel through the physical
To reach the other's other side,
As one about to die perceives
The further shore attainable.
Ovidius Naso breathed an air
In which the muses and the gods
Were coupling in the firmament,
Accepting ecstasy with ease
But always joined through metaphor:
There, seed was spilled in golden coin,
Or showering sunlight through a fleece
Of cloud, or ripples on a stream

(Streams like the rivulet which brought
Fresh leaves from Tristan to Iseut).
But Ovid obviously preferred,
To Heavenly bodies, those on earth:
The breathless summer afternoon,
The breathing presence giving forth
The warm geometry of bliss,
Uncurtained nakedness. And yet,
For all this physicality,
He still amusingly employed
Those metaphors of martial love,
The soldier's weaponry engaged,
The amorous sword with skill deployed,
Sweet conflict in the warring field.
And so despite his passionate art
Chaste curtains hang from certain lines;
And he from Tomis' distant shore,
Illustrious progenitor,
Must guide us when we speak of love.
Thus let our words be Latinate.

101

Beneath the shielding pine tree's arms
Armed Tristan lay with fair Iseut
Her face competing with her breast
For Tristan's adoration, thighs
Pale as her hair, like harbour walls
Seen at the mounting white wave's crest.
She cast aside the torn chemise.
And as she held to all the past
Entrusted to her in his face
And held him inextricably,
They found importunate in them
The impulse to be everywhere,

A craving to intercalate
A lifetime in between these days.
Intercolline his head, his face
Breathing her skin, her hands
Rejoicing in his back, they lay
On leaves, and felt the world as still
As buried leaves becoming coal.

102

The paradox resolves itself
In these terms: when Description turns
To details of the physical
And catalogues of nakedness,
It threatens those dichotomies
Of mind and body, flesh and soul,
The very same divisions which
Love unifies. Better to say
To him her body was the day,
A dazzling field of hills and sun,
An orchard filled with fruiting trees,
The possible in sweet undress;
And he to her the solid world
Which takes on form heroically,
A means of giving weight to speech,
A banner to be there unfurled;
But now a more immediate threat
To love's transporting joys emerged:
Sometimes the king hunted all day,
And knowing he was long away,
And with Brangain's help to allay
Suspicions at the brooding court,
Iseut the Fair, the Passionate,
By signs the stream arranged, could meet
Tristan by day, more daringly.

The barons watched but could not see
What still they sensed instinctively
From Iseut's face. Duke Andret said
– *The king is so besotted, mad
With love, his heart rules his head.
Look at the queen. Tristan has gone.
But still there's something going on.
What we can't prove there's someone can.
Send out and find the dwarf, Frocin.*

≈

103

– *The dwarf, Frocin*, cried Ganelon.
*Why didn't I first think of that?
Get him to wear his magic hat
And use his skills at sorcery,
The seven arts and alchemy,
And reading entrails, and the king
Will be undone.* When he sat down
Another jealous knight, Gondoine,
Spoke slowly to his audience:
– *I'd been about to say that too.
He's famous for his skill in trance.
They say he caused the earth to move
And leaves to fall from trees in spring,
Just by the turning of a card.*
Duke Andret anxious to be heard
Stood up and interrupted him.
– *I'll send my men to bring him soon.
They say he once exhumed a grave
And learned his secrets from within.*
Frocin was sent for. In a fen
At length they found him, setting snares
For leverets. But trapping hares
Could wait the pleasures of the court,

And Focin said – *I knew*
The stars conjoined suspiciously.
And now I see the fateful name
Of Tristan written in your heart.

104

A travelling malevolence,
Frocin arrived at court and spoke
To the unwilling king. So keen
Were all the knights in advocacy,
The king knew he had no defence
Against their villain. So, Frocin
Consulting charts, said – *Let King Mark*
Announce a week-long hunt and then
Set out with all his entourage
Loudly with cries and trumpeting.
And one day later, let the king
By stealth consult with me again.
Lay down these premises; engage
The syllogism Destiny;
And by the gods, I guarantee
A rare conclusion. Thus will our liege
Too soon find out what's what at court,
Whose stars are crossed, and whose are lost,
    And who's with whom entangled.

105

And now we almost reach the place
Where rain, mischance or avarice,
Or breeze at open windows or
The unknown stranger at the door,
Or gravity which lets it fall
Lost from the baggage of a mule,

Or fuel to kindle some hearth's flame
For a churlish servant lacking fame,
Or paper needed for a bill
Which caused a hundred more to spill
Before a careless notary,
Or lapping and voracious sea –
Whichever act beyond recall
Took those first pages of Béroul
And then desisted, leaving all
That now remain. Now let these sail
Across the intervening world
In safer breezes, all unfurled,
Perilous no more as those now lost,
And, blowing open, come to rest
In Tristan's pine tree – Even as
The king is led across the moors
By Frocin to this very place
And climbs the tree on his advice
And waits. There he may read Béroul,
Beginning with those dotted lines
For blurrings on the upper page
And see perhaps cold Fortune's rage
Against himself, Iseut the Fair,
And his Tristan, soon his no more.

106

Frocin had left the King alone.
The horses went with him. The moon
Was muffled in a sash of cloud.
Mark waited, hidden. Soon he heard
Tristan below the tree, and saw
Him reach to break a branch. He trims
And strips the bark from gleaming stems;
And floats them in the stream. Mark waits,
And Tristan waits pacing the shore.

Then Tristan bending at the pool,
Saw suddenly reflected, pale
As the moon, his uncle's floating face,
Troubled and faint, a shimmering trace.
He could not stop the reckless stream's
Too eager running to Iseut,
But he must wait, and know their fate
Hung in the balanced, branching tree.
He did not look up again. He met
The unaccommodating night,
With its indifferent moon, in which
They could not hide. Still he paced on
Until he heard Iseut approach.

107

Iseut came to their lake. Something
Was different; she sensed the king,
Or some pale thought of his, was near;
And Tristan did not run to her.
The night's protective cloak she wore
Was fringed with danger. Then the moon
Launched out from banks of ruffled cloud,
Sharpening the light, defining shade
Until, distinctly in the pool
She saw the shadow of the king.
She did not look up. But when Tristan
Approaches, she must be the one
To speak first. – *Tristan!* she said
Listen to me. What possible
Excuse could you have found to call
Me here at such an hour? The king
Should kill me if he found me here.
I don't know why I came – for fear,
Perhaps, or gratitude, since you
Did kill Morholt and bring me to

The king, my life. And here she wept
A little, then resumed. *Tristan,*
There are now many evil men
Who would delight to find me where
You see me now. But I can swear
That all their rumours are untrue,
That no man ever had my love
But he who had me as a maid.
So tell me what it is you need
To tell, and, for honour, let me leave.
Tristan now saw that she had seen
The shadow of the king above
And said – *My lady, as the queen,*
I ask that you should intercede
For me with Mark, our king. Your room,
My lady, is forbidden me. Therefore
I asked you here. The king, I fear,
Now hates me; why, I do not know;
But since you are the queen, I thought
You might gently prevail on him
For my unhappy sake. For, whom,
Chaste queen, could he trust more than you?
Iseut, longing to hold Tristan,
Yet stood apart and coolly said
I too have felt this sorrow. But
For his sake it has brought me pain
And since, Sir, I would rather burn
Than give myself to anyone
Than my true lord, I will not risk
Addition to his suffering.
She moved still further off. She turned.
A fire in her blood still burned
And yet she said – *Sir, do not ask,*
Or speak of this to me again.
        And so, Sir, let me go.

108

Tristan alone beneath the pine;
King Mark still clinging like a vine
In tangling branches overhead:
Stirring the pool, loud Tristan said
– Alas, the injustice of the world
That I by my uncle am reviled,
And by his wife, the purest queen
This troubled, treacherous world has seen.
Alas, Mark was unjustly right:
Already I have left the court
At his demand, not knowing what
I may have done and now I see
This land has nothing more for me
Than misery. And so I'll leave,
And travel far with no man's love
Other than loyal Gorvenal.
In some strange land, on distant soil,
I'll stand beneath this powerless moon
Which cannot choose if it would shine
Just as at court in Tintagel
I had no choice reflecting ill
From others. So he sighed again,
And left along the river plain.
The king climbed down. He cried aloud
– What treacheries have I allowed
By jealous barons and the crowd
Who swayed me to believe a lie
Which now was clearly false! I see
Prodigious error here. No man
May slander those I love again
Or taint Iseut and my Tristan
For now I'll punish base Frocin.

109

Frocin was in a copse of trees
By night, plotting the paths of stars.
Ascendant Venus and Orion
Conveyed to him the king's design
(For Frocin's powers were genuine)
To part his body from his soul.
He saw the king now reconcile
Divisions in the court, Tristan
Restored to grace. He saw Brangain
Commend the queen for cunning skill,
Tristan confide in Gorvenal;
And then, again, the stars reveal
The king proclaiming *Death to Frocin*
At which the dwarf fled into Wales.

110

The king woke from delicious sleep
And, for a moment, wondered why
His image in the frosted glass
Now smiled. Contagious happiness
Seemed in the air, as if the day
Were ushered in by Tristan's harp
As in the time of innocence.
He sought Iseut and said to her
– *My lady, answer this without pretence:*
When have you seen my nephew, he
Who slew Morholt and brought you here?
She felt a shaft of fear, immense
And chilling, ominous, and yet
As thrilling, hearing of her Prince.
She said – *I have not lied to you*
Nor shall I now. I saw Tristan
Last night. He sent for me. We met
In moonlit darkness at the pine.

My lord, I'll tell you everything.
He said – No, let me think – I said
– 'Tristan,' I said, 'You should not bring
Me here at such an hour. The king
Would not approve of it.' And then
I said, 'Tristan, let me return.'
And he said, 'Lady let me speak.
I suffer, through these jealous men,
The king's disfavour. Intercede
For me with him. My uncle Mark
Is misinformed.' And I said 'Sir,
We're mindful of our debt of care:
You killed Morholt and brought me here
To my fulfilment with my lord.'
And here I think I wept aloud,
And then I said, 'Don't ask again
Like this for me to take your side.
I will not risk more suffering
For the king.' That king cried out in joy,
– I heard you from that moonlit tree
Frocin persuaded me to climb,
I heard you say all you have said.
Iseut looked up – *You mean, my lord,*
You climbed that tree, you saw and heard
Our conversation? Then you know
That all I've ever said is true.
The king embraced her many times,
And said – *Our happiness, it seems,*
Returns. But Tristan vows to leave.
I must convince him of our love
And stay him and restore to him
        The freedom of our room.

Part Seven

111

No sooner had Tristan returned
To favour and the court, and moved
Once more in Iseut's waxing flame
Than he and she became more free
Than ever previously; restrained
Too long they now seemed openly
Aggrieved to be apart too long.
Some knights close to the king had come
Upon them naked in his bed.
Some said – *This cannot be. The king*
Must see the shame they bring the court.
If ever man and woman loved,
The queen and Tristan seemed intent
To better them in passion spent
And passion rapidly revived.
The knights in anger met. One said
– *The king must be informed, be made*
To see the extent of this excess
So blatantly displayed. Disgrace
Is overtaking Tintagel
And will destroy us all. One knight
Cried – *Let the dwarf return, and let*
Him use his powers to end this shame.
Much altercation followed. Mark
At length agreed – *I would not seek*
To lose my loyal knights for what
I thought already was disproved.
Again call Frocin, though I vowed
And still I feel, that he should die.
Frocin arrived, so soon it seemed
He knew this summons imminent
And hastened, anxious to be redeemed.
– *You've acted wisely calling me,*
He said. *I felt immediately*
The presence of a shameful lie.

112

With astrolabe and charts, Frocin
Was grave, a cosmic potentate:
— Venus is faltering, in decline.
Instead the warring planet, Mars,
Is governing the unruly stars.
But listen closely to my plan.
The time is right to ascertain
The truth about our young Tristan;
This paragon without a stain
Is just a comet burning out,
A trail of scattering ash. It's plain.
But listen closely. First the king
Must send his errant nephew on
An errand to King Arthur's court.
But do not tell him this until
The household's settled for the night,
That he's to leave by morning light.
Give him some letter with a seal —
Its contents can be anything —
To take to Arthur at Carlisle.
Now, Tristan sleeps beside your bed;
A long spear's length away, Iseut,
And others further round. Tonight
You rise and leave — make some excuse.
And soon we'll see how their excess
Exceeds all limits. He will cross
To lie with her, I'm sure of it
And I will prove it. In the dawn
You'll see it with your very eyes
Or my name's not Frocin the Wise.

113

King Mark agreed to everything
Drawn on inexorably like streams
Which cannot know of falls ahead.

Frocin has disappeared. The king
Speaks then to Tristan as he comes
Into the hall and to his bed.

– *Good nephew,* said the king, *the light
Of day must see you on the road
To the King of Courtesy at Carlisle.*

*Give him this letter and our heart,
And then return.* Tristan agreed,
But thought of fair Iseut and all

The hours of land and sky and trees
Which he must spend without her face.
He puzzled how he might greet her

Before this night was passed. He sees
The king rise up and leave his place,
And then the dwarf Frocin, with flour

Which by the candles' light he spreads
Across the floor. Tristan sees him
And knows the danger he must face.

A spear's length lies between their beds,
One print in flour must bring them harm,
A leap the only way to cross.

114

Frocin spread flour across the floor.
It lay untouched like winter frost.
Iseut was far from sleep. Their host,
The king, had left mysteriously.
As one who from a white chalk cliff
Looks on a dark tempestuous sea
Towards the isles of his desire
Tristan looked out from sheets of clay.
The floor was like a frosted field,
Or foam of waves the desolate coast
Throws back beneath an empty sky.
Frocin had left, and left Tristan
This problem. Could he make it yield
Solutions? How, if now he crossed,
Could he avoid marking this flour
Which spread like seeds in summer bloom
On weed fields stretching endlessly?
Perinis snored some distance off;
A calm had settled in the room
Except for two loud beating hearts.
And calm is far from Tristan's mind
And in his passion he forgets
The wound which only yesterday
A boar had opened in his thigh
Whose drying blood has not been bound.

115

Tristan leaped in a single bound
Across the spear's length ocean bed
To Iseut's bed. And there confined
By love's sweet bonds gladly assumed
He did not feel the opening wound
Or see the seeping, spreading blood.

Frocin was outside with the king,
And in the moonlight saw resumed
Their passion. Exultantly he cried
– *Sir king, bring in your knights and seize*
This king and queen of treacheries.
The king was sad, outraged, dismayed,
And even now thought everything
Might be delusive or a dream,
So calmly shone the indifferent moon.
But the knights burst in just as Tristan
Alerted by these vengeful cries,
Leaped back across the moonlit field
And lay amongst his bloodied sheets.
But on the floor their lights revealed
The scattered flour beaded and stained
By dark and copious blood, and on
The king's own tousled sheets, still warm,
And on Iseut's white arm, spread blood
While blood drained from these lovers' hearts.

116

Fate in a single bound now leaped
And seized Iseut and Tristan. Knights
In tumult crowded round the beds
And seized and bound them with strong cords.
They saw the blood where it had crept
Across the scattered floor and sheets,
Already hastening to congeal.
They urged the King to swift revenge.
Those knights who, jealous of Tristan,
Cried loud and with unseemly zeal
Which jealousy need not conceal,
Now jeered. And several drew their swords,

And one would, for the King, now plunge
It into Tristan's heart. But Mark
As fiercely spoke, ordering them back.
Tristan cried – *Mercy! Spare the queen.*
And then he said – *Noble King Mark,*
Remember I am of your blood.
Show mercy for our Saviour's sake
Who suffered in his Passion. Bring
Your heart to bear. Remember Him
Who for our overwhelming sin
Brought to our state forgiveness,
Who knew that He could have no choice
Upon this earth than that cruel Cross.
And equally for some of us
Who suffer in this time and place,
Who have no choice in how we are led
By blood or destiny, we need
To beg your mercy, sovereign lord.

117

Bound Tristan now was not allowed
Trial by conflict in the field,
And this because the barons feared
Their fear of him would be revealed.
And they had bound the king in ties
Of stable kingdom and the need
For retribution. So it was
That, without further trial, he made
His men prepare a ditch of thorns
And lay more branches over these
To make a pyre. Through all the towns
The cry rang out: King Mark was mad
With cruel rage. The people came
And at the court cried variously,

– The king is going to burn his wife
She who has been his love and life.
– And Tristan who once saved us from
The dread Morholt and Cornwall's pain,
The sacrifice which we were bound
To make. Someone must stay his hand.
– At least give them a proper trial.
– Iseut was always kind to me.
– Tristan is brave and fair. The knights
Who would not fight Morholt – let them
Speak out, tell who's behind all this.
– This is the evil of Frocin.
Someone should run a sword through him.
– What's in a kiss? It could be worse;
They could be cruel like Ganelon.
– The queen they say looks very pale.
And then the king spoke in a rage.
– My people, as I am your liege
I will decide what's for the best.
I want my peace. The die is cast.

118

A minstrel echoed their distress:

– The world is running down. The Hand
Which gave us motion, now
Retreats into a cloud. The dove
Is no more heard across our land.

The woods encroach, and wilderness
And vines now bind the aspen bough.
A dark confusion reigns. The grove
Is smothered in the weed's embrace.

So fiercely bound, Iseut's wrists bleed.
She weeps and cries aloud, 'A cloud
Covers the sun. The world runs down.
Our orchard soon is overrun.

Our pine tree is weighed down, alas,
And falls to an engulfing grave.
If I could die that you might live,
The afterlife would bring me bliss.'

But they have fallen out of grace.

119

Tristan was brought out by the knights,
Strong ropes about his pinioned arms
Which once were free to hold Iseut
But now must all forswear. The charms
Of yearning days and perfumed nights
Were past, lost from this envious world.
Iseut cried – *If it could be willed*
That I should die to set you free
I would thereafter savour joy.
But now to see you cruelly bound
Brings shame to all this barren land.
And still the king was adamant
And would not hear the populace
Cry mercy. But instead he went
In grave talk with the malcontent
Duke Andret at the pyre. Tristan
Was being led towards the fire
And had to pass a chapel spire
Which stood high on the cliffs. It faced
A chasm and beyond, the sea.
He felt the ropes round him enlaced;

He thought of nothing but Iseut
As one who travels through the night,
After long absence, nearing home.
He did not speak, savouring her name.
It seemed she walked with him within
These chafing bonds, and with his eyes
Saw at the towering cliff fresh hope.
Tristan addressed his captors. – *Sirs,*
The final fire is imminent.
I wish to pray within this church
Alone. If you will free my arms
I'll make my peace with God. For each
Must meet his destiny as he will.
I am unarmed. I can't escape.
This chapel has but one door. That
Ten knights should surely hold secure.
For honour's sake allow me this,
A moment's prayer before the fire.
The occasion favoured sober words;
The knights agreed – they had their swords,
And stood guard at the narrow door.
But once inside, without a thought
Of empty space that looms beyond,
He runs; he crosses the chancel rail,
Draws back the window's ruby glass
Behind the altar in the apse,
And to the void unfearing leaps.

120

Swallows against a blue sky.
Finches above a narrowing field,
Their sound like distant bleating sheep.
Another field racing below,
The peristaltic ocean wave.

Tristan was sailing through the air,
The sail an image of Iseut,
As air began its narrative,
A rushing history of love.
The air was like a shattered flask
From which have scattered everywhere
The dregs of some rare elixir.
Celestial in the blood their spray,
Breaking on beaches far away.
Perhaps the time is apt to ask
Who Tristan is and who Iseut,
If each lives in the other's thought
And knows no other selfhood now
Than what inheres by this exchange.
Perhaps to him it was Iseut
Who fell, who rose, who sailed, whose cloak
In billowing had stayed her fall.
Some say he landed in the sea
(If such a thing is possible)
And others that, miraculously,
As only fortune can arrange,
He came to rest in sand on stone
Through cushioning leaves which years before
Had spread themselves for this alone.
The place is still called *Tristan's Leap*.

121

To be precise about the time
And place, when Mark spoke to Iseut,
It was that dappling afternoon
When western trees hold back more light
And in their shade flowers begin
Slowly to close; the place, a room
Iseut had never seen before,

Somewhere secure in Tintagel,
Which looked out on a funeral pyre.
It was also the time Tristan
Fell slowly through the void, and saw
The history of the world unfold
And open like a rose. The king
Had come to her in sorrowing rage,
Resolved to punish her, unswayed
By the clamourings of his seneschal,
Though Dinas spoke persuasively
On her behalf, for clemency.
Iseut was bound. Her wrists had bled.
As shadows lengthened in the room
They spoke of love and treachery
And rage and sorrow. Iseut said
Much then concerning destiny,
A force that travels in the blood,
A reading hand which turns the page,
A wine which he, Mark, should have had.
The shadows fell as Tristan fell;
Along the shore came Gorvenal
And found Tristan and brought his sword
And brought also his coat of mail
And urged upon him caution – *Now
Is not the time to venture out,
For folly is not prowess. Wait.
Your men are scattered. You alone
Could not prevail against those knights
Who hate you. Wait instead for Fate
Who brought you safely down to earth
To make for you along this shore
      A path back to the queen.*

122

The thorns were burning, and the flame
Spread upwards through the scaffolding
When Dinas, Lord of Dinan, came
And threw himself before the king
And said – *I beg you to retract,*
And not pursue this course, this act
Of base revenge without a trial.
Relent, before it is too late.
The people say the evidence
Is circumstantial, merely blood,
That none saw an improper deed,
And many still believe the queen,
Condemned, they say, without defence.
Still others say it is Frocin
Who should be seized and burned. So, wait.
We fear that, spreading through the state,
A wave will gather to a flood
Of anarchy. The people know
That Tristan has escaped and will
Through all this wide realm generate
Support. He knows the country well,
The plains, the hidden passes, fort
And valley, peak and river flat,
And in each place he'll raise a force
Which will at last destroy us all.
And still the king could not contain
His anger and unhappiness
And brought Iseut before the flame.

123

And now the deepest wilderness
Encroached on these events. Iseut
Was led towards the mounting flame

And still the protests from the cloud
Rang out, just as the lepers came.
A lazar house, dark in the wood,
Divulged its dreadful occupants,
The lepers and those outcasts from
The walls of Tintagel, who lived
(If huntsmen were to be believed)
In tangled suppurating gloom
Where leaves on leaves decay and fume
And skeletal remains recede.
They seemed like creatures for whom time
Accelerates beyond all bounds.
Misshapen, frightening, odious
Like boughs grotesquely bifurcate
On certain trees deprived of sun
In overgrown, sequestered lands.
Yvain, their leader, shuffled to
The fire. His rags and skin alike
Seemed made of ancient manuscripts
A long time in the ground. He spoke
As one who shivers long in crypts:
– *Good king, we rarely leave our den*
To speak to normal folk like you,
But having heard of great events,
Betrayals and a burning too
We girded up our loins. Now Mark,
We think you've made a bad mistake.
If you burn fair Iseut you'll have
Mere ash. The punishment won't last
And this is why we now suggest
You give Iseut to us, to live
And lie with us, to guard and gird
Our loins, if you understand.
We take it you want her disgraced.
Well, let her beauty fade with us

In our contagious forest. There
We'll share her out; you may be sure
Her punishment will be most fair.
Iseut cried out – *My king, no more!*
And cried above the searing roar
Of fiercely burning branches – *Sir,*
Burn me, rather than condemn
Me to this lingering life in death.
A flame leaped like a jealous wraith.
Perhaps her cry, resounding still
Above its roar, or fear, at this
Consuming flame's finality,
Swayed Mark to say – *Yvain, take her.*
    Do with her what you will.

124

The sky was ripe with seeding clouds
Like glistening pomegranate, dark,
Compactly clustered, glowering,
Which spread, as late sun coloured them,
And then dissolved in rain. Yvain,
And crowds of lepers clamouring
To touch her, roughly handled her,
And forced her to the forest rim,
As Brangain once at her behest
Had been. To think that she, Iseut
The bearer of the blood which bore
Wine of the gods should here be made
The object of such monstrous care!
Now almost lost from sight King Mark
Surveyed the dwindling, dampened fire
In sorrow and, at last, alone.
The forest darkened. The rain increased.
There seemed as little hope as light.

She fell amongst the nettled shades,
But harsh Yvain still dragged her on
Until as fortune would decree
(And who knows if capriciously
Or, in this floating world of chance,
By calm and heavenly providence?)
They forced her down the very path
Of all upon this branching earth
Where Tristan and brave Gorvenal
Waited their opportunity.
There are, as Béroul says, those men
Who say that Tristan slew Yvain
And others, equally misled,
Who say Yvain was drowned by him.
The old books here include a scene
Of splendid carnage. But Béroul,
Invoking Tristan's courtesy,
Avoids such lack of charity.
Admittedly, his Gorvenal
Has cut a stout branch from a tree
And beats Yvain about the head.
But are these creatures not the means
By which Tristan at last regains
His thread of gold, Iseut the Fair?
And threats are largely all they need
To take Iseut and leave this glade.

Part Eight

125

The Morrois Forest welcomed them
With open arms. It seemed to know
Their weariness, their need for calm
And rest, after their long ordeal,
And had prepared a bed of leaves
Under a spreading elder bough,
As if these trees with their own loves
Had found this forest long ago.
One scarcely knew the season here.
The greens were brilliant; yet the red
Of leaves still held. Was this
The warmth of early autumn, or
As stillness lingered on the air,
Late winter passing into spring?
The trees, benign, in sympathy,
Kept all such knowledge from them as,
Exhausted by their treadmill days,
Iseut slept long on Tristan's arm.
Events had borne them like a tide,
As an ocean floods its estuary
And pushes drifting craft upstream.
The fearful smoke had cleared. The sky
Once more was azure, purposeless
And uncoercive. So, the trees
Stood round their peaceful citadel,
Their kingdom distant from their king.

126

The Morrois Forest, welcoming,
Scatters its leaves on cushioning ground
As Gorvenal leaves them to find,
Some distance through the silting woods,

A genial fletcher who provides
A bow of splendid arching elm
And two fine arrows tipped and fledged;
As well, a cloak of linen, edged
With flowers, for Iseut. Tristan
Takes bow and arrows and sets out
At dawn. White mist still hangs and sways
In curtains, veils half drawn
Across a stylobate of trees,
A frieze of figures like Iseut.
Two roe-deer, in the clearing, pause,
And Tristan slays them with that skill
Which long ago in Tintagel
   Announced him to the king.

127

And Gorvenal cooked venison
And, though they had no bread, nor milk,
Nor salt, and all their clothes were torn,
Their happiness could find no fault
With Morrois Woods. One day they planned
To walk towards the west all day
To see a sight Tristan had found
While hunting. On the way
They passed a convoluted cliff
Of crenellated rock as if
The world here gathered like some silk
Thrown down, a folded secret place
Pristine in lichen, ferns and moss.
Yet through it ran a narrow path
Which timid creatures of the earth
Had made. At length they saw
Spread out, looming, at length, a lake,
Bounded by conifer and oak,
As white at dusk as Iseut's face.

Towards its light they walked on still
Along its bright perimeter
Until they reached a reed marsh, where
They watched against the darkening sky
The water burning. So they stood:
The freezing water seemed to boil
With fire the ancients knew as Greek.
This was a sign, the lovers said,
Of endless love, unquenchable.

128

Meanwhile, the knights, dissatisfied
That Tristan and Iseut were still
At large, felt that the king demurred
At any plans to capture them
And bring them home in sombre shame,
As if he loved them both, despite
Their treachery to crown and state.
They sought Frocin and gave him wine
And gave him wine, until he was
Inclined to speak more recklessly.
– *My lords, I've sworn by sun and moon*
To tell my secrets to no man.
But Sirs, there are ways round all this.
As Midas, given ass's ears
By raging, vain Apollo, wears
A hat to hide them with his fears,
Alone of men his barber knows
And with the mounting need to tell
Someone or something, digs a hole
And tells his secrets to the earth;
At which the grass and reeds increase,
Swaying in the soft wind's breath
And whisper knowledge to the air.

So shall I now, my lords, confide
My secrets to the hawthorn air.
I'll put my head through branches there
And if you happen to be near,
Unseen by me, the other side
May bring you whisperings from the stars.
They gave him wine and led him on
And brought him to the hawthorn boughs.
He put his head amongst the flowers,
Like skies at night profuse with stars.

129

– Lords of the air, attend to me.
I've learned a thing or two or three
In Jupiter's ascendancy.
Between you, me and this bright bush,
The things I've read, in fallen ash,
Or rainbows on the sullen moon,
Would startle merely mortal men.
I'll tell you what the stars kept dark
About our much esteemed King Mark,
A dismal mark upon the page.
If you're the page at court, beware.
Be where you can't be made the thing
Of this, affection's endless spring.
Is he, or is emotion king?
The king dissolves and, looking on,
Becomes the glistening field, Tristan.
The king's another Midas too:
He needs to wear a spreading hat
To hide his temple horns at that
Warm April and the first cuckoo.
Lords of the air, breathe your fill.
In April the cuckoo shows his bill.

In May the cuckoo sings all day.
In June the cuckoo changes tune.
In July the cuckoo flies away,
But not for our King Cuckoo Mark.
There's more than this. The stars reveal
The king is jealous of his wife!
Let no one fearing for his life
Let sifting flour fall between
The beds of Tristan and the King!
I could go on. The air is fresh
And most attentive, standing still.
This song resounds from every hill…
But then a sudden shadow fell
Across the star-white hawthorn bush.

130

The king was standing with his knights.
The sky was interlaced with lights,
The hawthorn's tossing heads of snow
Were speaking. And he heard, below
The frothing skyline's azure blue,
A voice he loathed. He heard, then saw,
Where branches crossed with snowflake flowers,
Caught in the stars' interstices,
The poisoner of his peace. Mark stood.
He listened still. He drew his sword.
Perhaps he sundered head and neck,
Perhaps he parted soul from flesh,
Perhaps he struck before he spoke,
For as he drew out from the bush
His sword streaming with blood, he said,
While petals eddied on the blade,
– *Foul slanderer, Frocin, we knew*
Nothing you ever claimed was true.

*I climbed the tree because of you
And teetered, for your evil sake,
Above the limpid, guiltless lake.
And next, you tricked us with the blood
From Tristan's wound beside the bed
And forced my only love to flee.
Let Cornwall now rejoice to see*
      This end to calumny.

131

Midsummer Eve came to the woods
And passed without its ceremonies;
Iseut and Tristan saw the days
As days of sun or days of rain,
But all of these, despite their pain
Their lack of food, their clothing torn,
Were days of paradise. Alone,
Surrounded by their solemn trees
They rarely saw a traveller.
And still the Morrois Forest shone
And praised their exculpating love.
One day into their woods there came
A saintly hermit named Ogrin,
Who said – *My lord Tristan, repent!
The king has promised rich rewards
For anyone who seizes you.
In every shire the barons go
In search of you. My lord, repent!*
But Tristan cried – *Of what could we
Repent who have been given this,
A life, a destiny as one,
As one bound indivisibly
And driven by a singular past,
And brought to these extremities
As now you see here at Morrois,*

By magic, by a wine that was
Not wine but Nature's own embrace?
Then Ogrin answered – *Sir, alas,*
A prince and queen should be more free
Than serfs, of whom the very least
Is free, as all men are, to choose.
And so, Tristan, Iseut, relent!
Iseut fell down before his feet,
Her hair like winnowed fields of wheat,
– Good Sir, you could not understand
How guiltless innocence is stained;
Imagine one who breathes the air
And finds that, strangely, suddenly,
It has become a clear bouquet
Of flowers one cannot refuse,
And which, once grasped, have turned to ice,
Then, Sir, one breathes their dolorous scent
   And never more is free.
The hermit said – *Then, if you must*
Stay on here in our votive wood,
Far from the court, you'll need to hide.

132

Despite the animosities
Which flourished at the court, there was
One creature who was loyal always
To banished Tristan. This was the hound
Husdent, who at his side would bound
In joy, but now was always chained,
And pined and fretted for Tristan.
For Husdent once had freely run
And hunted on the open plain
Or in the woods with keen delight
Beside the horses, through the bright
And rapid glades of hare in flight

Or pounding stag. Then he would bring
The prize, after the galloping,
To his master Tristan and the king.
Now many in the bleak court heard
These growls and howls. The base knights feared
And thought perhaps Husdent were mad
And might attack them. And Mark thought,
Thinking of days long lost to night,
– *This dog is wise. This dog is right*
To cry for Tristan in this court
Who was the noblest, fairest knight.

133

The grizzly hound strained at his chain.
He howled and whined for lost Tristan
With tears and sighs, and would not eat,
Until at last each counselling knight
Urged him unchained. The king agreed.
– *He may still seek Tristan and lead*
Us to the fugitives. The hound
Looked up then paused, then ran unchained
Towards the room where Tristan, free
No more, in blood-stained sheets once lay.
The knights followed. Husdent as soon
Ran on out of the room and down
The path delighting in the hill
Which led towards the chapel, still
Alive with Tristan's scent. A pause
To check the air; the narrow doors
Swung open and with eager leaps
He found the window in the apse,
Squeezed through and plunged with grateful cries
Down perilous cascading screes
Towards those wooded estuaries
Where soon he lost his followers.

134

The sun was high when Husdent broke
Into the glade where Tristan hid,
Who heard the snap of breaking stick
And feared emissaries from the king.
Husdent ran to them, strong in joy,
Arching his back, stretching a paw
Against each face, licking Tristan
And leaping up prodigiously,
Making himself as serpentine
In rapture as a threshing eel,
Twisting his body and his tail,
Turning in circles, following
His tail with panting, clamouring breath.
And written in his hazel eyes
The reassertion of that grave
And passionate, engulfing love
Which Tristan and Iseut sustain,
Suggested, as some men have done,
In long forgotten histories,
That Husdent too had been on board
That ship from Ireland, and Brangain
Had poured, for Husdent too that wine
Which brings the many into one.

135

When Husdent broke into the glade
Where Tristan hid, he barked aloud
And these cries echoing through the wood
Alarmed Tristan lest someone should
Be attracted here and find their bower
And bring those instruments of power
Which would divide them. So, Tristan,

Even though he shared the keen
Exultance of Husdent, must find
Some way of silencing the hound
So that the two may hunt, while yet
Not giving any venturing knight
Within these woods the slightest sign
That here, near sheltering oak and pine
Lie lovers in their troubled bliss.
Iseut said – *Sir, consider this:*
I heard once of a forester
In Wales who liked the forest air
To close round him in silent calm,
As silent as the glistening stream,
Who trained his hounds to quell their barks;
Admonishment and gentle strokes
Achieved it, so they say, in weeks.
Here, even as she spoke, Husdent
Leaped up and licked her face, and sent
A cry of rapt, loud loyalty
Into the echoing air. – *We'll see,*
Said Tristan, *if it's possible*
To teach our loyal animal
The silence of the shallow stream,
To answer to his whispered name
In kind. I'll find a distant glade.
Then, if we're heard, we'll still elude
The encroaching knights. Husdent will help
The hunt, without a single yelp,
You'll see, fair queen. We will succeed.
Through grazing glade we'll glide unheard,
Unseen, and track the browsing stag
With Husdent, our eloquent, silent dog.

136

To train Husdent in silent joy
Made Tristan and Iseut both sad
And happy, for they saw that they
Must silently seek joy here, clad
In rags, without a scrap of bread,
Without the company of the town.
And yet Husdent brought happiness
For, as he learned to hunt and run
In silence, so they smiled at this
And Husdent eased their loneliness.
And often in his eyes there passed
An understanding of their plight,
That bliss which like a harness forced
Itself upon them, that dark fate
Whose noon was like a starry night.
And so they lived on in their trance
And Tristan, hunting with Husdent,
Seemed in a kind of silent dance.
Through grass and ice and snow they went
In search of deer. But accident,
Which masquerading destiny
Invents and hides, would intervene
And end this endless reverie.

137

There are some incidents which seem
To need the darkness of a dream
As if the sun in fuming shade,
Eclipsed, behind its stifling cloud,
Would not cast light on such a scene
(Dregs still of that entailing wine)
As in the forest now befell.

Alone and sombre, Gorvenal
Was cast in sorrow and regret,
Feeling the lovers' trembling doubt,
The doubt which each must surely feel,
Each fearing lest the other fail
In resolution in this place,
Which writes doubt in the other's face.
He heard an uproar in the brush:
A stag pursued by dogs, the rush
Of cries and horses, then a pause;
And then a single horseman rode
Urging his mount, spurring its side
Until it stumbled and fell in pain.
It was the evil Ganelon,
That hated knight who had inflamed
The king against Tristan, who roamed
Now alone, without his horse or squire.
The glade seemed very dark. Power
To alter fate beyond recall
Fast flooded over Gorvenal.
This knight had never known remorse;
Just now he'd cursed and struck his horse –
So Gorvenal seized his sword and struck
Within the darkly glowering brake
The neck of this, his master's loathed
And vicious enemy. He breathed
Again as Ganelon breathed no more,
And sunlight ventured once more there.

138

But meanwhile Tristan reeled in sleep
Fearing Iseut must tire of him;
And fair Iseut, held on his arm,
Feared that the hardships for her sake

Might rob Tristan at last of hope
And love for her. And Tristan stirred
In anguish at the gulf he made
Between Iseut and once loved Mark.
They woke to find, in that pale glade,
Their lives, by loyal Gorvenal,
Placed even more beyond the pale.

⁂

139

Because the death of Ganelon
Made many fearful of the wood,
They saw no one. The sky was clear,
The breeze soft and beguiling there.
Midsummer wreathed across its brow
A tangled honeysuckle air.
They saw the distant harvesting;
They thought more gently of the king.
And one day, in the summer heat,
From hunting an elusive hart,
Exhausted, fainting, at his return,
Tristan fell to the grateful sward
To lie beside Iseut, and sleep.
The air was warm. Nevertheless
These lovers sleeping chose to keep
Their clothes about them; and they lay,
On this most fateful summer day,
With Tristan's sword between them. And
The queen still wore the emerald ring,
Mark's gift, although her fragile hand
Was thin and frail and scarcely could
Retain the band. These things we stress
Because such future happiness
As might be theirs will now depend
On all that Mark may shortly find.

⁂

140

Escaping from the shadeless hour
A forester had wandered deep
Into the leafy Morrois wood.
By chance he found the lover's bower;
He saw the emerald ring, the sword
Dividing their oblivious sleep,
Their faces close but far apart.
And so he ran, betraying love,
Considering always his reward,
Through forest almost impenetrable
Which gave at length upon a grove
And then to the towers of the court,
Where urgently he sought the king.
The king in conference said – *We are*
As you can see in grave debate
On lofty matters of the state.
What is your grievance? – Sir,
The woodman said, catching his breath,
My Liege, your vengeance is at hand,
And my reward. For I have found
The two whom you have sought. The earth
Is holding them for you. Your blade
Must soon despatch them. Follow now
While still they sleep. The king
In flowering rage drew him aside
And said – *Where are they? – Sir,*
They are asleep in Morrois Wood.
Mark said – *Tell no one what you know.*
Go; wait at the Croiz Rouge, near
The gravemounds. Wait and do not stir.
The king went to his knights, forbade
Them now to follow. But they said,
– *The king must never be alone.*

The bravest king must learn to fear
The dangers of the afternoon,
The jealousies which here beset
The court, the hidden sword, the deed
Sudden and irreversible.
The king replied – *My friends, a girl*
Has sent for me most urgently,
But asks me, in that urgency,
To take no one. Therefore I shall
Ride out alone. But all averred
– This is a matter for regret.
For even Cato urged his son
To avoid the desolate and solitary place
And everywhere seek company.
– I know of Cato, said the king.
But, even risking your distress,
I must insist. Leave me. Alone,
Unseen, I must now do this thing,
This thing in which I must not fail.

141

The sun looks through the heavens' gate
Into the wilds of Morrois Wood
And sees a figure, resolute,
Determined, on the forest path
Which leads across the turning earth
To where the lovers, sleeping, wait.
The stars consulting with the past,
The earth fast travelling round the sun,
The world revolves till, uppermost,
King Mark is striding through the fringe
Of oak and aspen, soon to plunge
Into that tangled thicket, Fate.

A voice was carried on the breeze:
*The sun moves through the poplars' height
The better to attain the sight
Of King Mark in the woods, alone.
The earth revolving round the sun
Enmeshed with all its unseen stars
To celebrate their measured dance
Brings Tintagel to prominence.
The sea, attentive at its shores,
The chorus of the attendant trees,
The air, all gathered to ensure
That nothing untoward will stir
The fringe of eyelash, closing eyes
In sleep, against the advancing sword.*

The planets in dark space revolved,
The floating stars were dutiful,
The sun converged on Tintagel,
As round it thoughtful clouds devolved.
The ocean like a cloak was pressed
About the sleeping, white-limbed coast,
As through the forest King Mark strode.
He reached the place where dappling shade,
Like light reflected on a wall
From running water, stressed the pale
And unfamiliar faces there
Of Tristan and Iseut. He came
Towards them, thinking of their shame,
With upraised sword about to strike.
A spiralling cloud of birds, their shriek
Dismissed by distance and the breeze
Above the massed, protective trees,
Saw Mark approach the bower. Soon
Iseut would lie with her Tristan,
And lie to all the world, no more.

142

With unsheathed sword the king drew near,
His rage already mixed with fear
That something unexpected here
Might put him from his purpose. Fair
Iseut was sleeping. Golden hair
Like threads of interflowing air
Half strayed across her face. She stirred.
The two lay close. Yet something stayed
His arm. Perhaps he understood;
For there he saw the naked sword
Between them lying on the sward,
A sign which everyone may read
As symbolising chastity.
And they were clothed! And he could see
No hint of sensuality
And soon he thought: Might it not be
That banishment had cruelly
Condemned them to this life, that he,
The king, was wrong! Chastely they lay.
Between them shone the burnished blade.
They lay, divided, courteously.

143

At this, the earth abruptly slowed
Its headlong passage round the sun,
And stood a moment to regard
Its present light. The king's arm weighed
More heavily with its upraised sword.
He must not touch them, even wake
Them from their pastoral sleep. Instead
He felt impelled, in this chaste shrine,
To exchange his sword for Tristan's own
Marked by the shard which Morholt took.

He claimed the sword and left that one
Which moments earlier should have slain
The lovers sleeping, undisturbed.
And as his anger eased and ebbed,
The earth stood still one moment more;
A shaft of sunlight found a way,
Through overlayered oak leaves, to
The leafy bed where Iseut lay,
And formed a pool upon her face.
The promise of great happiness,
Her beauty, still shone out. And Mark
Drew off the ermine gloves which she
Had brought to him from Ireland; these
He hung upon the shadowing tree
To shield her from the burning rays.
And finally he took the ring,
Which easily slipped from Iseut's hand,
And left another in its place.
Nothing is quite as we have planned;
The world resumed, without a trace
Of this delay, its onward course.
The sun moved in the sky. The king
Walked back to mount his tethered horse.

144

And Mark dismissed the forester
Who waited at the forest road,
And said no more of his reward.
Many at court sensed in his air
Abstraction, reverie, a mood
Of guarded secret happiness.
And when they asked where he had been,
He lied. Such questioning, such duress
He answered vaguely: in the wood
He travelled but had seen no one.

145

Beneath the canopy of leaves,
Through which the sun shone fitfully,
Iseut and Tristan moved through sleep.
Another sword between them lay;
Another ring upon her hand,
Above her face the ermine gloves,
All waited their awakening.
But the queen was entering on a dream.
She stood within a royal tent,
Hung richly with embroidery,
In some vast forest. Next she went
Into a lion's lair and there
She stood, replete with curious hope,
At which two lions, famished and
Desiring her, stood at her side.
She felt fear wanting to cry out,
But ardently the lions roared
And took her hands. Her waking scream
Woke Tristan, as the white gloves fell
(The way a leaf knowingly falls)
Across her breast. They woke. They saw
The ring, the sword with unscarred blade,
They recognised the pommel's gold.
And when they knew the king had come
And held his sword and yet withheld
The fatal blow, they feared the gales
Of fortune blowing through their lives.
They feared and puzzled, reasoning
That, knowing where they slept, the king
Would soon return with many men
To capture them and seal their shame.
They summoned Gorvenal. In haste
They left and travelled to the west
And through the Morrois Wood to Wales.

Part Nine

146

For many weeks they suffered still
The conflicts, sown like dragons' teeth,
Of love and honour, sacrifice
And freedom, joy and pain. The earth
Appeared indifferent. Tristan
Observed the shortening days which soon
Would bring again the swords of ice.
The western woods were dense and cruel,
And fear, which gathered to a knot
Impelled them daily. On and on,
Through thickets where the taloned thorn
Tore their clothes, they pressed. That heat
Alone, still burgeoning in their blood,
Sustained them in the Morrois Wood.

147

A field of foxgloves, overgrown,
Now welcomed them, a flowering town
Amongst whose towers they could rest.
This day, a subtle change occurred
But one which was at first obscured:
The Queen of Ireland had expressed
An elixir from curious plants
And passionate ingredients,
To burst from their efflorescent wine
To seek two hearts: *Iseut, Tristan*.
Now, on this day three years had passed
Since Accident, through frail Brangain,
Had claimed them. But they had not known
Three years would see its power gone.

148

The elixir had lost its power,
Or so the manuscripts relate,
But might not Tristan and Iseut
Quite fail to recognise the hour?
For in their blood these potent lees
Had spread inland like neap-tide seas
Which override sea walls, and flood
The coastal groves and estuaries,
Orchards and fields, the frothing glade,
Then, drawing back, leave sediment.
Just so, might mutual content,
Habituation, courtesies,
And real affection have ensured
That passion, once induced, endured?

149

Tristan was hunting when it came.
He stopped. He let the deer escape.
He seized the moment shaped like ice.
This glacial moment did not pass.
With it he hastened to Iseut
And in her arms she welcomed him.
He said – *The woods were set alight,*
The sun spilled out deliberately,
And all the gilt trees spoke to me.
I feel as if we were asleep.
For this life clearly is not fit
For you. But why did we embrace
This life of suffering, without a thought?
You should have lived at silken court.

150

– You should have lived at silken court,
Surrounded by your ladies, not
Condemned by me to nettled groves
And settlements of foxglove leaves.
You should have been in Beauty's lists,
Or coolly in a curtained room.
The world of men, lashed to their masts
As you passed by, should sing your name.
– And you, my lord, surely you should
Have been in sumptuous ermine clad,
Triumphant at love's tournaments,
Heroic at the battlements,
Winning my husband's gratitude,
Seeking and claiming high reward.

151

– My lady, you to whom I gave
My life, and always to whom love
Is due, and given, for my sake
I would desire you reconciled
In honour, with my uncle, Mark,
In his benevolent ambit held.
And if he would at last believe
That never did we knowingly
Love with dishonour, then, for me,
There would be no knight in the land
From Lidan hills spread like a hand
To Durham wound upon a stream,
Who would not find my willing arm
Upraised, should he impugn your name.

152

– *The forest now is, we agree,*
Abhorrent and insufferable.
Today the trees stared down at me,
Or past me, like a dark blank wall;
The gorse bird vanished as I turned,
The rocks and stones seemed more concerned
To billow in their solitude
Than to yield space to me. This hard,
Harsh place which once seemed beautiful,
Which once, to our embrace, seemed royal,
Now robs our people of their queen.
But, at the hermitage, Ogrin
May intercede for us and seek
Our restitution with King Mark.

153

Searching for Ogrin in the wood,
United by the search, they shared
A kind of tender happiness.
And when the forest gave upon
A long neglected orchard, there
They saw spent apples weighing down
Their willowy branches and, below,
Red fruit already globes of wine,
Half covered by long spears of grass.
They feasted on this sweet repast,
As bitter-sweet seemed all their past
And sadly joyful their embrace.
At last they found the hermitage
As Ogrin, reading, turned the page.

154

The hermit cried out, offering praise
At their repentance of this sin
While offering them more food and wine.
– My friends, I'll help you if I can.
You're welcome at the hermitage,
And here we'll plot what's best to do
And say, to remedy this thing.
We'll write a letter to the king.
Repentance lets us, in my view,
Invent appropriate falsehoods. Oh!
Let us praise this turning of the page
In that eventful book of days
Which endlessly we write. But, now
To work, my friends. Where were we, then?

155

– I'll cut this piece of parchment, thus.
What must we say? We start, of course,
With greetings from you both. Or should
We stress at once your great remorse?
My friends, you've asked for my advice
And I shall give it. Let us say
That you are in the woods this day
And if the king should wish it so
The queen is willing to return.
And you, most honourable Tristan,
Would swear to serve him if you could.
That you escaped from fire and sea
(I mean in leaping from the cliff)
Shows God's good grace on your behalf.

156

These things and many more were tried,
Fresh parchment cut, still more ink brought,
The single candle flickering
Burned to a sputtering pool, before
This work was at an end. They sighed
In weariness. But Tristan said
— *Add this: that I still fear the king*
Who put a price upon my head.
We ask him to reply, and bring
That to the Croiz Rouge. This was done,
The letter sealed with wax and set.
Then Tristan said — *Before the dawn*
While fair Iseut sleeps in your care,
I'll take our letter to his door.

157

With Gorvenal, Tristan set out.
At parting, Iseut's eyes were bright
And lingering. The way was dark;
The dangers on this path were great.
Dismounting high above the town,
He went in stealth and passed the guards
Whose mournful trumpets told the hour.
How different were the town and woods,
How dark the king's remembered tower.
He called and tapped the window. Mark
Cried — *Who is that? Speak your name.*
— *I dare not stay. It is Tristan.*
I leave this letter to your fame.
And Mark cried — *Wait. Wait. Do not fear.*

158

And Mark cried – *Tristan, do not go.*
Tristan! Nephew! But Tristan's fears
Were real. Already he had gone.
And, following the flush of dawn,
He left the dark town far below.
Iseut's eyes still were filled with tears
When he arrived. Then while Ogrin
Gave thanks for Tristan's safe return,
The king was reading yet again
That letter which, the following day,
Would test his barons' loyalty:
– *My lords, hear what we now propose,*
The vindication of Tristan,
The restitution of the queen.

159

– *My lords, I've asked you here today*
Because I value your good will
And all that you might have to say
Concerning this. This letter, seal
Intact, reached me some hours ago.
I duly bring its text to you.
The Chaplain read, persuasively,
… *The king's indebtedness; a plot;*
The lack of proof; the enforced flight;
The obligation to Iseut;
Tristan by honour bound to right
This wrong; threat to the state;
In reconciliation, late
Better than never in God's sight…

160

The king cried – *Well, my lords, now speak.*
Then Dinas rose and said – *Good Mark
And noble lords, if what we've heard
Is true I see it as the time
Of Cornwall's healing, and I would
Most strongly urge Iseut's return.*
But others said – *Let not Tristan
Return with her. At least let him
Serve overseas, in Brittany
Or far from here with Galway's king
Who fights the Scots. And let us see
A year of her fidelity
Before we risk the further wrong
Which Tristan's presence here might bring.*

161

As eagerly as Mark could write
His joyful letter of reply,
Tristan was pacing through the night
With his Iseut (who hid her sigh)
And Ogrin (who with lengthy yawn
Would have preferred to sleep or pray).
At midnight Tristan left. He ran
Through forest paths which he alone
Knew like the maze of hair which fell
Across Iseut's fair face. He took
The letter from the crossroad's cross
And ran back to the holy place:
*Iseut is reconciled to Mark;
Tristan must other Kingdoms seek.*

162

Ogrin served them with pallid wine,
Re-read the letter several times
And several times enlarged upon
Its clear import. But to Iseut
And enervated, pale Tristan,
It signalled parting. Nothing more
Held meaning there. No other claims
On their attention reached that heart
In which the threatened edifice
Of all their life, like glacial ice,
Stood in this letter's sun. They spoke
Of Tristan on a distant shore,
Iseut borne on a flood bound ark
Paired with one other, worthy Mark.

163

Outside the hermitage the sky
Was dark and still. There was no sign
Of dawn. Iseut and Tristan walked.
Iseut said – *Just as Dido ached*
For lost Aeneas, so shall I
For you, always. Alas, Tristan!
Do this for me: leave me Husdent.
No one could be more provident
Than I in caring for him. When
I see him leaping, my despair
May pass. And, Tristan, in return
Take now this jasper ring, and wear
It always. If you should send this ring,
I will be held back by no king.

164

The Markets at St Michael's Mount
Were known to be the richest source
Of silk and linen, perfume, spice
And every finery, in the South.
The hermit bought there, for Iseut,
Deep purple silks with subtle scent
(Which were the finest on the earth
Ogrin was told), a linen, white
As lilies, and a length of bright,
Red damask. Next, he bought
A palfrey decked with gilt-edged cloth.
And thus the queen might meet the king
And show no sign of suffering.

165

When Tristan and Iseut rode out,
All Cornwall wished to see the queen.
On every side, pavilion
And banner filled the meadow lane.
In haste, reaching the appointed line,
She cried – *Tristan, I beg you, wait*
A little. Do not leave this land
Until my fears are at an end
Concerning the king. Stay nearby
At that cottage where we often met.
There may be knights still who would try
To act against us. He took her hand.
– *I swear it on this jasper ring.*
And now they saw the approaching king.

166

While Tristan held the queen's rein,
The palfrey paused. The king came out,
A bow-shot from his loyal men.
With him was Dinas of Lidan.
With careful courtesy they met;
Tristan, acknowledging the king,
Said – *Sir I bring to you your wife,*
Whom I have guarded with my life.
But here I must request the right
Not yet accorded me, to meet
In field and court those who would wrong
Me still. But several knights demurred
And said, drawing the king aside,
– *Tristan must leave. We were agreed.*

167

– *Take gold and silver,* said the king.
But Tristan said – *Not any thing,*
I take nothing but memories
Of days and nights near Cornwall's seas.
And as he turned and left, Iseut
Stood watching him until he was
Crossing the meadow where the crows
Wheeled always, then a fleck, then mote
Which she would not put from her eyes.
The king perhaps had shared her tears
But spoke with kindness, waiting then
For Dinas who had ridden out
Some distance to the furthest lawn
And talked in parting with Tristan.

168

The bells were ringing in the town
As Dinas parting from Tristan
Returned and joined the king and queen.
The town was filled with revelry.
Each street gave banners to the breeze,
Each window showed its tapestry
And, at St Samson's church were strewn
Rose petals for the queen. She came,
And joyful people called her name.
Outside the church, where all could see,
The bishop stood in alb and cope
While abbots carried reliquaries.
The queen put on a dark blue cloak
And stood, like gold, beside King Mark.

Part Ten

169

When the escorting barons left,
And Tristan travelled on alone
He turned at once into a lane
Which led back through the forest gloom
Towards the woodman's hut. Diffuse,
The dappled light and shade streamed down.
Tristan spoke softly to his mount
And bent towards its mane. Low boughs
Passed overhead. He heard the sighs
Of falling water. Soon he saw
A fountain curving from a cleft
Low in the cliff, beside the pool.
He watched this curving plume perform
An endless repetition. First
The arc of water caused a wave
Which washed back then against the jet
Which caused it. Where these currents met
The water whitened. This in turn
Confused the long collapsing arc
Letting the wave subside, and thus
The restitution of the plume.
Tristan looked down. He watched this grave,
Perpetual machine at work,
And spoke as softly to his mount
Who grazed and moved on fitfully.
Tristan was in a reverie;
His grazing, fitful destiny
Bemused him. All seemed like this sluice
As if events were liquid, held
In some uncertain high borne bowl
Tilting between extremes. The past
Pressed forward through the arching trees.
And even as he lingered here,
The king conversing with his knights
Was once more entertaining doubts.

170

The woodman, Orri, who in the past
Befriended Tristan and Iseut,
Now welcomed Tristan to his hut.
Where they had lain, now Tristan lay
Alone, waiting, in troubled rest,
For Perinis with word from her,
Who sweetly, in this very room,
Had taken him into her heart
And turned the troubled world to calm.
Meanwhile the king faced several knights
Who pointed out that still, by rights,
The queen should prove her innocence,
That he, the king, should now demand
(To meet the clamours of the land)
That she produce in her defence
Some proof, or meet some public trial
Or test by suitable ordeal.

171

The king, enraged by this, so soon
After the joy of these rich days,
Spoke angrily to those three knights
Who argued so persistently.
*– You claim to stand for justice, yet
You stubbornly would not agree
That Tristan should defend her. So
It was when Morholt raged at large,
And none of you, who speak of rights
So loudly, would defend our state,
And all was left to brave Tristan.
I do not any more believe
You want my happiness. This love*

Is like a stumbling block for you.
He scarcely could contain his rage
And threatened to recall Tristan
Heaping on him unbounded praise
At their expense. At this impasse
The king withdrew. Feelings of loss
And anger showed upon his face.

172

Iseut was frightened by that face
Which spoke of some discovery -
Perhaps of Tristan at their hut,
(Perhaps he had now found Tristan)
And so she fell into a swoon,
And lay before the startled king.
But he embraced and kissed Iseut,
Reviving her. – *I feared*, she said,
The huntsmen had distressed my lord.
He smiled and said, now earnestly,
– *Our joy, it seems, must have its price.*
Three evil knights harass me still.
They spoke of you. I should recall
Tristan to drive them from our land.
– *My lord, what do they say of me?*
– *They speak of uncorrected wrong,*
They say that you must vindicate
Yourself in public, show at last
That past denied and laid to rest.
Iseut said – *Why do they persist?*
And yet I'll meet these Cornish men;
But it must be in my own way.
The king cried – *When may this trial be?*
I'll need, she said, *some short delay.*

173

— It must be done in my own way.
But Cornish men are prey to doubt.
No proof can ever be the last
For them. Therefore, my lord, we must
Ensure that all the world is there
When that long day's events declare
My innocence. Let us invite
King Arthur and his knights, Sir Kay
The seneschal, Gawain, Gerflet…
My lord, let runners bearing praise
Beg them to leave their Table Round;
Appoint a time in fifteen days
That all our doubting knights may meet
Upon the fields of Blanching Land.

174

The queen called Perinis to her side.
You will be asked to go, she said,
To seek King Arthur in Carlisle.
Go first to Tristan in the wood.
Speak of me gently. Then recall
To him the marsh near Heath of Sand,
Near which there is a wooden bridge.
(Remind him how one day I fell
And slightly soiled my dress. He will
Remember that.) Tell him to go
Early that day along the edge
Of Blanching Land. Say he must wear
The garments of a leper, and
While sadly seated on the mound,
Must carry in his blemished hand
A drinking cup, and hold it near
His pock-marked face, for alms. (He may

Be even given silver by
King Arthur and his knights.) Tell me,
When you return, all that you see.

175

The proclamations were declared.
The disaffected knights returned.
Perinis left the woodman's hut
And spurred to seek King Arthur's court.
Near Stirling Wood a minstrel sat
Beside the road, playing a flute.
King Arthur and his knights? he said.
Why, Sir, they are quite close at hand.
You'll see a tower and a hall
And there a turning table, vast
And turning like the world, where all
His knights in conference gravely sit.
He thanked the minstrel, and soon had passed
A double avenue of oaks,
And through their arches several lakes;
Almost at once Perinis found
The castle with its tower and moat,
And crossed to sunlit courts. A knight
Conducted him to Arthur's side.
– My lord, we crave an audience;
This horseman galloped through the land
Most urgently to speak to you.
Perinis thanked the knight and said
– God save King Arthur and his court.
I travel from the Queen Iseut –
The king cried *– You are welcome here*
And doubly so because your queen
Is as beautiful as hawthorn boughs
Or crocuses in winter snows.

How many times in recent years
I've tried in vain to hear from her.
Tell us her message now. Speak.
Perinis told that company all
The tribulation she endured
And of the evil knights who fought
To plunge the sword of dark discord
Between her and the king. He named
The offending knights. He spoke
Of vindication and the day
On which Iseut asked them to be
At Blanching Land. The king exclaimed
That he would bring a hundred knights
To Blanching Land, to guard her rights,
To ensure the fairness of the trial,
To witness carefully the defence
Against those barons' perfidy.
– Take greetings to fair Iseut;
Tell her that we agree with joy.

176

Gawain leaped up and loudly claimed:
– I know these barons you have named
And I would gladly see them maimed
In jousting or in tournament.
Gerflet was eager to agree:
Why, one at least is known to me.
I jousted with the villain once
And I would hang him from a tree
With my own hands with half a chance.
King Arthur said – *Well, gentle men,*
We'll have some jousting for the queen,
At Blanching Land. Against this day,
Ensure your horses are as sleek

As are your swords and shields. And dress
With that particular finesse
Which characterises Arthur's court…
And now, good Sir, join us and eat
And then I'll ride part of the way,
At least beyond the furthest oak,
And we can talk about your queen.
Such beauty now is rarely seen;
A man on horseback might do worse
Than speak of it. They say she's like
The sun above a misty lake.
But what of Mark in all of this?
Perinis turned and reined his horse.
– Alas. It must be said that Mark
Is always all too easily swayed.
He's like an aspen not an elm,
A ship with several at the helm;
He shifts like shadows on the sea
And changes for affection's sake
Pleasing no one. Then Arthur spoke.
– I know, myself. Excess of tact
Can make it difficult to act
Decisively. But tell your queen
We'll be there with a hundred men.

❧

177

The earth turned in its slipping track,
A cartwheel spinning in the mire;
And like those doubts which smothered Mark,
It cast its shadow on the moon.
Beneath this hand the night was dark;
An owl could scarcely see to fly
And Iseut waited for the day
At Blanching Land, when all would see

The exculpation of the queen.
For fifteen days the moon moved on
And out of shadow into light
To mark the day when all convene
At Blanching Land. Tristan, disguised,
Approached the bridge at Heath of Sand.
His shoes were patched. He wore a cloak
Of coarse, dark wool which he had charred
And dirtied in an open fire.
He seemed to limp and lean. His skin
Was soiled and marked and deeply scarred.
When he had gone to Gorvenal
That loyal man who knew him well
Was hesitant to let him in,
So far from being recognised
Was scrofulous Tristan. And they'd laughed;
But Gorvenal was anxious lest
Iseut should give some overt sign
Which others saw. But Tristan said,
– *We who live by shadowy night*
And have concealed a thousand pasts
Are careful always. Look! My sword
Beneath these rags. But now, my friend,
You must yourself be wary too,
And bring my horse to Blanching Land,
Who is as white as a comet's tail
And therefore must be cloaked and left
Nearby, but hidden, near the ford.
You know where it is easily crossed.
Avoid the marshes at all cost.
And hide there too my lance and spear;
I may contrive to conjure fear
In several barons in the lists.

178

The earth turned in its slipping track
And underneath the radiant arc
Of heaven, arched above the land,
A beggar sat upon a mound
Above the bridge at Heath of Sand.
On every side the marshes lay;
Few men but he could find a way
Across this slough of seeping clay,
Its hidden drifts of quagmire, lace
Of glistening and deceitful gorse,
An archipelago of moss
Where tiny beetles walk on pools
And sinking ground prepares for fools.
Already on the higher ground
Bright billowing pavilions lined
The jousting field. That beggar smiled
To see the first foolhardy knights,
Away from their familiar courts,
Urging their mounts down from the field;
With reckless cries they reeled and lunged
And into sinking quicksand plunged.

179

These knights were Tristan's enemies,
Amongst them those who plotted his
Division with the king. One cried
– *Base leper! Tell us if this mud*
Will ever end. And Tristan said
In rustic tones – *Spur on your steed.*
The ground is firm at bottom, Sir.
That knight rode further in, so far
The dark mire rose above his knee.

And all that proud knight's battle dress
Was soiled and splattered with marsh mess,
His noble cloak beyond recall.
Tristan enjoyed this spectacle,
And struck his alms bowl with his staff.
But no one there could see him laugh,
He huddled so lamentably,
Except Iseut approaching by
The bridge across the sullen stream.
And she laughed too to see that fuss.
The knight rebuked him – *Varlet, why
Did you pronounce the bottom firm
When all this place is endless foam?*
– *Why Sir,* the beggar, querulous
And whining, said, *Why this abuse?
You've just not reached the bottom yet.
Give me your hand.* But when the knight,
So much despised, slipped from his grip
And fell back down the greasy slope
Into the mire, the beggar said
– *I'm sorry, Sir, my arms aren't what
They used to be. But when you're out,
You must put something in my cup
And give the suffering world fresh hope.*

180

And soon King Arthur, man of myth,
Not straying from the tested path,
Came riding, with his retinue,
As fine as lawn in glistening dew.
Superbly elegant in blue,
He passed the beggar on his mound,
And Tristan asked with outstretched hand,
His voice well muffled, strained and hoarse,
For some small token from his purse.

At this the king reined in his horse
Caparisoned and splendid. – *Sir,
He said, Poor suffering creature, where
Have I addressed your like before?*
(Except that he was tall and free.)
The noble king gave generously.
And later when King Mark rode by,
Tristan, with trembling alms bowl, stood
And Mark drew off his ermine hood
And gladly gave him that and said
*– With this I wish you happiness;
The weather here is treacherous…
But Sir, how came you by this curse?
– If only I could tell you this.
They do say, Sir, the intercourse
Of lovers can afflict the blood.
The husband of my mistress sowed
Its seeds and I inherited
Through her this malady. Ah well,
You could say, Sir, she turned my head
And turned my head to what you see.
My lord, I say this seriously,
She was, without the slightest doubt,
As beautiful as fair Iseut.*
At this Mark smiled and rode away
Past floundering pools where knights, astray
In mud, were struggling to climb free,
Obliged to shed their finery
And shiver, like a windswept tree.

181

As Dinas winked, passing Tristan,
Iseut dismounted gracefully
With one hand holding her gentle mount,

And with an expert ease secured
The saddle cloth, so that the fringe
Would not be soiled or stained. With that,
She sent the palfrey through the stream.
Now hear at last of her intent.
(But, first, hear how the queen was dressed:
A swathe of gold across her breast,
A cloak of precious Baghdad silk
And under it as white as milk
A tunic made of finest lawn
And over this a waisted coat
In several shades of heavenly blue.
Her hair was tied in a melange
Of linen bands worked in gold thread
Which made her seem more radiant.)
And standing near Tristan she said,
So clearly all the world might hear:
— *You there, seated on your mound,*
To reach that firm, dry, stainless ground,
I need your help. You there, yes you,
Listen to me. All this occurred
In front of Arthur and his men
And Mark and many servants, all
Alert in curiosity
To see Iseut speak with this man.
And next they gasped to see her climb
Upon his shoulders and entwine
Her legs about his neck. He bent
Under her weight. He crossed the bridge
Of broken planks and creeping sedge.
And then she whispered in his ear,
— *Appear to stagger with my weight,*
Stumble and fall. They reached the edge,
And on dry land the leper fell
And for a moment lay between

Her legs. There was a general cry
At this great impropriety;
Onlookers hastened forward. She
Stood upright. She thanked him distantly.

182

The sun stood high above the Heath
And, robed in long judicial clouds,
Looked down in judgement on the earth.
Iseut asked Mark now to begin
The process of swearing on
Whatever relics might be found
Or brought here by the populace,
To answer all her inquisitors
Might ask of her. Meanwhile those lords
And kings, who saw the leper fall
And lie between Iseut's white thighs,
Slow falling with her to the ground
For just that time it takes a leaf,
Turning, to fall from sky to turf,
Before he rose with clumsy grace,
Now drove him off into the wood.
Iseut said – *Do not beat him, Sirs.*
He suffers. He is as harmless as
A sudden fall of summer hail.
But masters, may we not proceed?
A cloth of dark grey silk was brought,
Wrought with strange embroideries
Of animals in attitudes
Of penance or devotion (bought
At great expense for Arthur's court
In Palestine or Babylon).
On this were placed the reliquaries,
In order of their rank and state:

Gold crosses and an amulet,
A goblet and an ancient phial,
The leather-bound phylacteries,
A casket of obsidian –
All these were laid out on the grass.
Iseut knelt at this portative shrine
Like buildings scattered on a plain.
Then Arthur, always voluble,
Said to King Mark – *Behold this sward*
Equipped to validate the word
Of Iseut who is most willing here
To swear. Now let us hear the oath.
Let her stand forth and, without fear,
Holding her hand above the cloth,
Denying all wrong-doing, speak.
And once this deed is heard and seen,
Let no more malice come between
The state of Cornwall and its queen,
Or fair Iseut and wavering Mark.

183

She stood, like some exquisite deer
Confronting an adversary,
Its eyes the colour of the sky
Which, even as it tentatively
Raises one hoof but does not flee,
Darkens with its approaching fear.
She stood with one hand raised. She praised
The sacred relics on the cloth
And said – *My lords, I shall take the oath.*
But first she cast from round her neck
The heavy jewels (gifts of Mark),
Then slowly took her ermine cloak
Her mantle and her overdress
From her and cast them down. She stood

With arms and feet quite bare. She mused,
– *My lords, I stand before you here*
As naked as the king would wish,
Facing your judgement, fair or harsh,
Deprived of all the signs of power
And earthly riches. Now let truth
In all her nakedness stand forth.
By all the saints, by Holy God,
By all these relics and by more,
Scattered and lost across the earth,
(And here she spoke with melting sighs)
By perils I must face, I swear
That no man lay between my thighs
Except this leper whom you saw
Protect me from the marsh, who fell
While carrying me across this ford
And fell across me without sin,
That poor, weak creature, and, of course,
My husband Mark, the Virtuous.
And this, I swear before you all
And on these holy sacraments,
Is all. All those who heard cried out
That such exquisite innocence
Should not be punished further. Still
She knelt and softly prayed until
King Arthur and her husband came
And raised her up and spoke her name
And said – *Iseut the Fair, your fame*
Must evermore be without stain.
And Arthur said – *Fair queen, trust me.*
For I am now your surety,
And shall ensure that Mark trusts you.
She thanked them deeply with her gaze.
The sun shone calmly. Free from fear,
The deer once more grazed peacefully.

184

The sun shone fiercely. In its light
To let all Cornwall celebrate
The vindication of Iseut
King Mark decreed that every knight
Enter the lists, and take his part
And joust to win his lady's heart
In joy. Tristan and Gorvenal
Had dressed themselves deep in a vale
And now rode thunderously into view,
Tristan in black, riding Bel Jour,
The finest horse one could procure
In all the land. And blazoning too
Upon his lance his lady's plume,
He loudly challenged all that court.
And Gorvenal, cloaked all in white
With glittering arms, rode without shame.
Gawain cried – *Who are these who come?*
And Gerflet said – *I know them well.*
That one in black is known to call
Himself the Black Knight of the Hill.
They have no equal in this isle
And are enchanted, I have heard.
Gawain said – *We shall see.* Indeed
That company soon would see, for hard
Upon that solemn ceremony,
A merry melée would decide
Some reputations and some heads.
For enemies of Tristan went
With honoured knights into the field
With many loud and boastful words
And talk of great, heroic deeds.
And Tristan entering the fray
Saw, from the corner of his eye,
The treacherous Andret suddenly
Strike basely at him from the side.

Tristan wheeled round and dealt a blow
Which Andret might, if fortunate,
Remember many a year. And so
The fortunes of the tournament
Ebbed there as gaily as they flowed
Until in victory Tristan turned,
While other knights, unseated, reeled;
He saw Iseut, behind a veil
Still visible. He saw her smile.
And Tristan turned, with Gorvenal,
And galloped back into the woods
As rapidly as he had come.

185

That night the king dreams fitfully:
His queen has sworn on reliquaries,
Yet certain skeptics in the crowd
Have challenged her to undergo
The Ordeal by Iron. Willingly
Without delay, she smiles, agrees
And goes to where the brazier flares.
A sword is plunged into the coals
And left until it is as red
As breasts of tropic birds. Her smiles
Bring all of Cornwall to these halls
To see her exquisitely seize
This red hot sword. Mark sees her fears.
The day is cloudless. And yet she
Is held in such affection by
The natural world that as she stares,
Out of the cloudless sky there comes
A sudden deluge locally,
A rain which floods the brazier flames
And quenches there the waiting sword.
She holds it up triumphantly.

Part Eleven

186

And now, at last, we see, alas,
The Kingdom of Past Happiness
Dispersed, the last clerestories,
The palisades, the libraries
Of former joy, the dome, brought down,
Perhaps for ever, in dull pain.
When Arthur left for Durham town
And Mark and Iseut sailed a sea,
Torpid, with neither breeze nor sun,
Nor any unfamiliar shore,
And Tristan went to Brittany,
His love a fallen fruit, its tree
Bent under rime and lichen, all
That once was bright and bountiful
Dispersed and vanished from the earth.
That Alexandrian library
Of bliss, burned down and buried, now
What stunted trees may grow again?

187

Tristan, in Brittany, employed
As mercenary for Duke Hoel,
Was welcomed for his fearless skill
Against invaders from the west.
And, fighting to forget the past
He fought alongside Kaherdin
Who was Duke Hoel's only son.
And, all this time, his memory
Was like some dark sarcophagus,
Or body wrapped in linen cloth
Which every day seems to increase,
Detail grown fainter every day.
By trying to forget the earth

Had ever brought forth Fair Iseut,
Already distanced, Tristan had
Forgotten much he must forget,
Until its essence all was lost.
Just as the ancients once had thought
That honey fell from cooling air,
(And even Virgil spoke of leaves
On which the sky cast sweetness down),
So Tristan found within his heart,
So heavy with its weight of care,
Those empty, devastated hives
Which once had welled with nectar. Now
No sweetness swelled his heart. Tristan
Grew more and more oblivious
Of all that once he knew as bliss.

ಎ

188

Once, in the woods Tristan had heard
A mournful cry, a strangled word
Which, following, he found a stag,
Its antlers tangled in a tree
Which bent to hold it. Suddenly,
(And he could not himself set free
As he had freed those twisted flanks),
He felt from himself such antlers grow
To tangle in the branch filled sky,
As if he now were Acteon
Turned to a stag for having seen
Artemis bathing. And he longed
For those fierce hunting dogs who thronged
Round Acteon to end his pain.
He felt the roots grow from his brain,
Felt branches blacking out the light.
Then one day, much surprised, he met
Iseut With Hands of Snow. She was

The sister of brave Kaherdin.
She was, were Fair Iseut not born,
As beautiful as a summer rose,
And when he heard that name's strange power,
He felt drawn to this lesser flower,
And spoke in sleep the name, Iseut.

189

The enemy repulsed, all Brittany
Rejoiced in this stranger from the sea.
Tristan felt little in their praise.
As aged Diogenes had seen
When Alexander blocked the sun,
A shadow grew across his days.
Inured, Tristan was now like one
Who sits within a garden wall
Until the sun at last must fall
And in that fringe of shadows move
The spectres of one former love
Which vanish in night's darkening wave.
But in these shadowy days he saw,
And in his darkness did not see,
This surrogate Iseut. And yet
He sought the company more and more
Of this Iseut With Hands of Snow;
By virtue of her presence here
She grew upon him. Soon he could
No longer separate her charm
From all that flowered in her name.
At length, relentless destiny
Drew breath and dived into this sea.
Kaherdin lay awake one night
And heard Tristan cry out – *Iseut!*
And loving both, misunderstood.

190

Duke Hoel, welcoming this news,
Was overjoyed. Iseut, his child,
To wed this Tristan who had foiled
All their invading enemies!
Tristan was startled, then agreed.
She was as fair as anyone
Could be, not being Iseut the Fair.
For Tristan was as vague as air,
And easily found that he desired
This sweet named creature. And he would
In every likelihood not see
Iseut the Fair again. And she
Must surely be allowed to be
At peace with Mark in Tintagel.
Such veils were added to the veil
Which passed between him and the world.
In everything his judgement failed.
To live for love as he had done
Only to have the world move on
And take the world from him – no one
In these unknown extremities
Could ever know himself again.
But speculation on this strange
Estrangement from reality
Through love that only could derange
Might fill a thousand palimpsests,
Each one erased repeatedly;
Suffice to say Tristan agrees
And henceforth takes, like Hercules,
A life of Herculean tests.

191

A mist was lifting on the fields.
A scree of wrens with flittering cries
Flew back and forth, faithful in pairs,
Between iced trees and frosted folds
Of fallow ground. This wedding day
The Druid stones stood sombrely
Where Tristan walked alone. The sea
Seemed not to want to take him back.
He leaned against a standing rock
And felt the flow of something rare
Like currents in impending air
Which sharpen all the senses, yet
Decline to be explicit. These
Effusions from the ancient leys
Spoke to him of his destiny
Could he but hear them. But
They sounded far too distantly
For Tristan, distracted and remote.
The wedding day dawned bright with joy,
Its preparations underway
As Tristan wandered in the wealds.

192

That night his squires attended him
And, drawing off his nuptial sleeve,
Preparing him for pale Iseut
Who waited in their bridal room,
The fair embodiment of her name,
By accident dislodged the ring
Of jasper from his hand. It fell
And, on the floor, resounding rang
So that, aghast, fearful for love,
He shuddered at this wedding night.

193

The bed was all in ermine dressed
For pale Iseut With Hands of Snow.
Her ladies enviously withdrew,
And Tristan lay on finest down
Beside this fresh, entrancing name.
And through her silk, enruffled gown
Laid open at her swelling breast
He saw a landscape undulate
Under a fall of snow as white
As were her hands. All should he seek,
A flower of the field to pluck,
A prize which every man might claim,
And yet he lay, in faint perfume,
In silence. After a troubled time
Iseut spoke – *Sir, is something wrong?*
Have I displeased you in some way?
By now Sir you should be the king
Of my affections, I the field
And all these territories be held.
But Tristan said – *It is the pain,*
A wound from long ago, which healed
But has not healed. The fault is mine.
Fair girl, were I another man,
You would not still be languishing.
But keep our secret. Let us wait,
Sweet friend. This pain may soon abate.

194

Blackbirds were calling from the trees
Compiling lengthy inventories
Of who did what and where this day.
The afternoon was still and clear,

Made for such confidences. Here
Kaherdin and his sister rode
Beneath these trees. Then in their shade
They galloped through a shallow ford
Fringed with obsequious willow wands.
Where water ran through snow white sands
The horses' hooves in glittering pools
Threw up a hand of spray. It swells,
And breaks and splashes on the thigh
Of pale Iseut, reaching so high
Beneath her skirt that she cries out
– *What forward water, bold and bright*
More than my lord, importunate
To touch these parts which no man yet
Has known. And overhearing this,
Kaherdin reined his prancing horse
And seized his sister's reins, and said
– *Dear sister, what have I just heard?*
Iseut replied – *More than I should*
Have said, and then in tears, their mounts
Grazing together, without pretence
She told of Tristan's reticence
And all these days of her distress
To wear each day the veil and dress
Of one who is no more a maid.

195

Confronting Tristan, Kaherdin
Spoke fiercely on Iseut's behalf,
Rebuking Tristan for the shame
Which he would bring their family's name
And swearing on his very life
That he must challenge Tristan, who
Refused to make Iseut his wife.

Tristan sighed deeply – *If you know,*
If you would listen to a man
Whom destiny has cast ashore
In endless exile from his heart
And made a living man no more –
But leave your knights and ride apart
All day with me, and you may hear
The very history of pain.

196

He told him of the elixir,
Of how he drank of love and death,
As one who drowning drinks the air,
Tossed on the ocean's breast; of Mark,
And treachery by knights and dwarf;
Of meetings by the orchard lake
With her in whom he seemed to dwell,
Her name perpetually on his breath;
Of separation and its harm;
Of life seen as one long farewell;
And how Iseut With Hands of Snow
Had, by her very beauty made
Him know he could not live this life
In exile. Then he tried to speak
Of all which he had not before
Considered or attempted. So
He told him of strange memory
(It was the elixir of course
Which even now refused to fade)
Where blades of grass, an insect's wing
Which fell once on the outstretched arm
Of Fair Iseut, all such detail
Of Anything and Everything
Which ever happened in her gaze

Or with her, he remembered still.
And even more: he could not doubt
That things she'd seen but he had not
Were held in some periphery
Of his elusive, painful thought –
And thus the fear of action, which
Should crowd his teeming memory
Already overfilled with her...
They passed beneath a copper beech
Metallic and unreal. They slowed,
Then stopped. Beyond them, in the world,
The berried thorn-trees lined a field.

197

This left Kaherdin lost in thought
And as they passed the copper beech,
Returning, he said – *Why, of such*
Long litanies are martyrs made.
(I say not whether I mean those
Who listen long or who propose.)
But I will go with you to sea
To see this famous queen, that you
May know if she is true or not,
And, if the latter, you may return
To my Iseut with greater heart.
And so it was that they prepared
A coracle with two small sails
And left (with Gorvenal, and one
Sole equerry for Kaherdin),
Disguised as pilgrims, wearing cowls.

198

But now, Iseut the Fair, before
Her mirror, cried – *Two years and more*
Have passed without a single word
From him. I have not even heard
If Tristan lives or loves. And still
I am as constant as the mile
I walk along each day, that aisle
Of trees down which his absence floods.
The bee returns from distant glades
To hives deep hidden in the woods.
No one observes it in its cell,
And yet the hive must overfill;
So I am filled with love for him,
A nectar made from air and time.

199

A knight whose most heroic deeds
Were less of action than of words
(And often in his lady's room
But rarely on the field) now came,
And, lingering with Iseut the Fair,
With honeyed words spoke of the care,
Warmth and regard he felt for her,
How precious was the very air
She breathed, how wondrous was this trance
He felt. But her indifference
Led him into malevolence,
Regaling her unwilling ears
With tales of faithless love, of years
Of cruel neglect, of all he'd heard
Of one particular: Tristan,
The nephew of the king, now gone
From all his former paramours

To wed Iseut With Hands of Snow
In Brittany. – *Of course*, he said,
I am above such gossip. I
Speak only of that you already know.

200

Then Tristan felt against the hull
A current move, as if a wave
Had broken at the harbour wall
Some years before but, since that time,
Had waited, gathering strength from love
And from the turning treadmill sun
Each day while waiting to return.
Tristan was carried by its force;
The sail filled gladly. And their course
Seemed almost not to need his hand
Against the tiller. Then as dusk
Stained all the sea with shimmering musk,
Through dark, protective cliffs they came
Reaching the harbour of Lidan,
And gratefully resumed the land
Where all his heart lay. Towards the dawn
By fortune's flare they met Dinas
At crossroads on the castle road.
(Some say he slept astride his horse
Returning from his mistress' bed.)

201

The sun was rising through a mist
Which hung on branches iced with frost.
He welcomed them with joy, but said
– I beg you, for all Cornwall's sake,
Do not disturb the queen. For Mark

*Has reached a sort of happiness
With her. And she, perhaps, is calm.
And danger waits you, should you seek
To meet her.* Tristan said — *But why
Else should I come to Cornwall's shore?
Take her this ring. I urge you, show
Its jasper to her secretly.
Say that, whatever she has heard,
I have been faithful. Find a way
For me to see her. Ease my heart* —
— *Sir,* Dinas said, *in three days' time
The queen will travel from the court
With all her retinue; and where
The road divides to high and low
Near Blanching Land, there you can hide
Amidst the thorn bush growing wide
And see the progress of that sun.
Remember she is well attended. Yet
Within the castle where she'll stay
You may contrive to speak to her
Through some disguise or stratagem.
Meanwhile, stay at Lidan. But, Sir,
This enterprise I dread and fear.*

202

That all this world might rise again,
Tristan held hope dark in his heart;
And yet its course must take it soon
Into the shadow of the moon
Eclipsing all that might have been.
Already he saw its cold fringe
Of shadow into which would plunge
This travelling earth of stone and sky
And frail affections, courtesy,

And passion, gold in rift and vein,
And all past hopes piled like a cairn.
They waited in the thorn bush. Bright
The glittering of the cavalcade
Approaching down that double road:
The heralds; a minor dignitary;
Stewards; the sweepers of the ground;
The cooks and bearers of the cups;
Marshals and huntsmen; priests in copes;
The masters of the hounds, each leash
Taut with its proudly prancing hound;
And falconers, a hooded bird
Indignant on each wrist; the crush
Of barons jostling to be near
The king high mounted on his steed.
        And then the ladies came.

203

Kaherdin saw the fairest form
That any man had ever seen:
Riding a dappled palfrey, she
Was radiant with complicity
Which seems to ask the very air
To share her thoughts. She smiled
And, with a bobbin which she held,
She wound a skein of silken yarn
Between her outstretched hands. His heart
Felt pain, a longing for the world
This vision seemed to advocate.
He whispered – *She must be the queen!*
But Tristan smiled at once and said
– *No. That is Camille, her maid.*
The long procession moved on still.

And then Kaherdin saw the face
He'd often seen, carved, high above
The altar rail, a gentle grace,
Perfection which demanded love,
Abstracted, in a reverie.
This face beside her cloak was pale.
Kaherdin said – *At last, the queen!*
But Tristan whispered – *No. Brangain,
As loyal as she is beautiful.*
Kaherdin gazed again. And then,
And then, he saw the doting sun,
And bending branches at her side,
And swallows darting in the air
As dolphins gather in the sea
Around the mariner. And then he knew
This was the queen, without a doubt,
More beautiful than his Iseut
More lovely than the loveless moon.

204

Three days before, when she and Mark
Were playing chess, Dinas had come
And, managing to make a joke
On King takes Queen, he had disturbed
Some knights and pawns, tilting the board
While pointing with a hand which bore
The jasper ring. – *Forgive,* he said,
*This thoughtlessness, spoiling your game.
Those knights should have been doing more
To guard their king from base attack;
And bishops too I saw, remiss
In their responsibilities.
They shared, perhaps, my carelessness.*

At this the king with pleasantries
Departed. Then Dinas described
The road dividing at that place
Where now sunlight advanced her face.
The queen had seen the jasper ring
And now she studied grass and ground
And, falling back behind the king,
She paused, dismounting where the road
Diverged beside the thorn trees' shade.
She found the branch of hazelwood
About which woodbine tightly clung
And in that sunlit air she stood
To hear the sound of finch and lark
Which trilled with skill from just these trees.
At this she cried aloud – *Sweet bird,*
Sing to me still at dark Lidan;
Mark rides ahead to Blanching Land
And I this night must sleep alone.

205

As if each were the other's self
They met and spoke again, at which
The pain of parting overtook
Their joy before it had begun
And yet that joy was exquisite,
Precious, compelling and complete,
As much because it could not be,
As that it touched that mystery,
The person, indivisible,
Who seeks division there to give
Provinces of the self in love,
While sensing too the imminence
Of that long wished-for severance
From all that binds the physical.

Where, in a room, a tapestry
Depicted ancient scenes, oblique,
Perplexing and yet lyrical,
Joyful Tristan, and Kaherdin,
Sat with Iseut for radiant hours,
Their friendship inexplicably
Sealed by the beauty of the queen.
They spoke of distance and regret,
The pain of passing, providence,
The power of names (as in *Tristan*,
Conferring sadness at his birth,
The double echo of *Iseut*),
The beauty of the shadowed earth,
Of lives as fragile as the air,
Of sailors tossed on fortune's seas.
They saw their interlacing past
Like fields razed by a sudden gale
Where houses, still precarious,
Once entered fall about them. Thus
There flowered in that curtained room
Foreknowledge that this was the last
Night Tristan and Iseut might gaze,
Which coloured all that gaze might yield
And raised them, soon to leave this world,
To grave and all embracing joys.

206

The old books urge this principle:
Such sombre endings should be told
Without elaboration or
The pomp and choral ceremony
Appropriate while hope remains.
But fear, sheer danger and the thought
Of rumour threatening to the queen,

Made it impossible to stay.
And so Tristan, in his distress,
Left Cornwall's shores before the dawn.
All was resolved, forgiven, healed,
That is, all that was once that past,
Which waited her absolving grace;
The many-sided die was cast.
But nothing could from them withhold
The cold, capricious wave which might
Break on their future. Soon Tristan
Again in granite Brittany
Lay with Iseut With Hands of Snow,
As if a sword between them lay.

207

In Brittany again, as sad
As fabled Afric crocodile,
Its fertile tears flooding the Nile,
Tristan by loyalty was led,
On loyal Kaherdin's behalf,
To skirmishes within a court
Which he had never seen before,
Where for the honour of his wife,
A knight attacked them vengefully.
While Kaherdin was grazed, Tristan,
Distracted by a blaze of light,
Was wounded by a poisoned spear,
And fell into a fever. Soon
He knew that he could not be cured,
Except by Cornwall's queen, she who
Had overcome Morholt's dark blade
And worked her magic long ago
Against the dragon's pestilence,
Who still was trustee of his heart.

Weakly he said – *Dear friend, if chance*
Were ever pleased to smile once more,
It would be by your speed: go now.
Sail back to Cornwall. Seek the queen.
Take jewels. Seem a merchant. Show
Them precious silks and gold, and so
Contrive to show the queen this ring
Which many times has travelled far
From that most precious hand on earth.
Remind her of the oath we swore,
The cup we drank to life in death,
And tell her I am dying now.
Beg her to come. Tell everything.
(But tell your sister nothing. She
Knows nothing of that mystery.)
Go now. But take two sails, one white
To set and billow joyfully
Above the curved horizon if
Iseut has come who heals the world,
Or black, proclaiming through the surf
That all is lost, that you have failed.

～

208

Kaherdin left without delay.
Outside this room, against its wall,
Iseut With Hands of Snow heard all
That had been said. She loved Tristan.
She understood. She wept. Each day
As, in a fever, Tristan slept
And woke, and floated in a world
Between two worlds, his fate unfurled
But waiting for a breeze, she wept.
She bathed his body, cooled his face.
And sometimes she would gently kiss

With tears his hands or lips. And thus
They waited in this Stygian glade,
And thus she suffered silently
The pain of love, that loneliness.
In Cornwall, fleeting Kaherdin
Brought silks and jewels to the court
And in the window's flattering light
Showed these to Fair Iseut alone.
He showed her then the ring and spoke
Of all that Tristan bade him speak.

Iseut With Hands of Snow bent low
And kissed his face with heart of ice;
She felt the sands freeze in the glass.

In Cornwall with a billowing sail
Like summer clouds, as white as snow,
The ship set out. The breeze stood fair.

209

Each day, as day and night confused
And interflowed like estuaries
Where tidal streams merge with the seas,
And Tristan in bright darkness lay
He asked if she would look to sea.
Each day Iseut With Hands of Snow,
Cooling his forehead, sadly said
– *The wind blows foam against the wall*
But no one comes. The sea is grey
Like ashes thrown across the land.
Each day he woke and tried to stand,
And asked – *Is there a sail? Look now.*
And then one morning, when the breeze
Blew gently from the sea, she gazed:
Her brother's ship came into view,

Its tilting prow she recognised
And watched approaching under sail
As white as hands of snow. Tristan
Called faintly – *Can you see her smile?*
Despite herself, and secretly,
Already filled with shame and fear
She heard herself coldly reply
– *There is a sail above the keel*
Far in the distance; in the sun
The sail is billowing and black.
At this Tristan fell fiercely back
And in a Stygian darkness saw
Black sails approach that river's shore.

210

The ship was curiously becalmed
Some distance from the shore. The air
Was still. They heard a tolling bell
Until the breeze again resumed,
And waves once more seemed to propel
Them into land. Iseut the Fair
Stepped on to Breton soil. She heard
A clamouring. An old man said
– *Lady, we suffer sorrow here.*
Tristan, who was so loyal, is dead.
And those who saw the startled queen
Said to each other – *Who has seen*
Such beauty, or ever one so pale?

211

She found the room where Tristan lay
Where, by his side, his wife in grief
Mourned what she had done. Iseut the Fair

Said – *Lady, rise and let me kneel*
Near him, who loved him more in life
And now in death than you could know.
Outside, the tolling of the bell,
While here, she lay. She kissed his mouth,
And took him in her arms, took earth
Soon to be earth. Then breathlessly,
They both lay still, made one in death.

212

Hearing these things, Mark crossed the sea
And came at length to Brittany,
His ship set with an azure sail.
He carried them to Tintagel
And gave them solemn burial
Within St Samson's church. The nave,
Some say, seemed filled with light;
And others say that from each grave
There grew a tree whose branches met
And intertwined above the aisle,
Filling the vaulted arch. And when
Three times the peasants cut them down
Three times their branches grew again,
Until Mark ordered they remain.

www.ingramcontent.com/pod-product-compliance
Lightning Source LLC
Chambersburg PA
CBHW050355120526
44590CB00015B/1700